# BON APPÉTIT
# 30-MINUTE MAIN COURSES

# Bon Appétit

# 30-Minute Main Courses

## from the Editors of Bon Appétit

Condé Nast Books ∾ Pantheon

NEW YORK

For *Bon Appétit* Magazine
William J. Garry, Editor in Chief
Laurie Glenn Buckle, Editor, Bon Appétit Books
Marcy MacDonald, Editorial Services Manager
John Hartung, Editorial Production Director
Lisa Davey, Editorial Coordinator
Selma Brown Morrow, Assistant Food Editor
Marcia Lewis, Editorial Support
Katherine Poyma, Editorial Secretary
Jennifer Rylaarsdam, Research

For *Condé Nast* Books
Jill Cohen, President
Ellen Maria Bruzelius, Direct Marketing Director
Lucille Friedman, Fulfillment Manager
Patricia Van Note, Product Development Manager
Thomas Downing, Direct Marketing Manager
Jennifer Metz, Direct Marketing Associate
John Crutchfield, Direct Marketing Assistant

This book was produced and created by
Joshua Morris Publishing, Inc.,
355 Riverside Avenue, Westport, Connecticut 06880.

Designed by Laura Hammond Hough

Front Jacket: Swordfish Steaks with Mango Salsa (page 89).
Title page: Fontina, Onion and Goat Cheese Pizza (page 46).

A cataloging-in-publication record has been established for this
book by the Library of Congress.
ISBN: 0-679-44220-0

Manufactured in the United States of America
FIRST EDITION
2 4 6 8 9 7 5 3 1

# CONTENTS

# INTRODUCTION

For the last four years, we have been writing the column, "30-Minute Main Courses," for *Bon Appétit.* But we have been cooking 30-minute main courses a whole lot longer than that. Like you, we have lives that stuff about a week into each 24-hour day, which leaves us no time to stuff a turkey or even a chicken for that matter. Our solution to this familiar problem? Meals made quickly with quick-cooking fresh ingredients.

Suppertime always seems to come at the worst time — at the end of the day, when everyone's tired and hungry. And between juggling jobs and families, we never seem to have much time to think about what's for dinner before dinner. In the past, we tried the take-out route (too expensive) and the cook-it-ahead route (too organized) and the see-what's-in-the-fridge route (sometimes little more than cold air). Now we have an arsenal of easy main-dish recipes that cook up in 30 minutes or less, making Tuesday at 6:00 P.M. in our houses a much nicer place to be these days.

As professional food writers and personal food lovers, we aren't willing to sacrifice taste and quality for time and convenience — a stance that pretty much defines our philosophy behind these recipes. In marrying that ideal with the constraints of time, we have found that it's the ingredients (and whether or not they are in your cupboard, refrigerator or freezer when you need them) that are the key to quick-cooking success.

All of our recipes are based on the ordinary ingredients and high-quality convenience products we describe in some detail in the pantry section that follows. We firmly believe that no one should ever spend more time shopping

Chicken Braised
with Bacon and
Potatoes
(page 60)

## The Cupboard

Artichoke hearts
Beans: black, white and kidney
Breadcrumbs, unseasoned
Broths: chicken, beef and vegetable
Capers
Chilies: mild green and jalapeños
Chili sauce
Chocolate: unsweetened, semisweet
Clams (canned) and clam juice
Coffee: regular, decaf and instant
Crackers: plain and graham
Dried fruits: apricots, cranberries,
    raisins
Extracts: almond and vanilla
Flour: all purpose
Herbs: basil, dill, oregano, rosemary,
    sage, tarragon and thyme
Honey
Ketchup
Maple syrup
Marinara sauce
Mustard: Dijon
Nuts: almonds, peanuts, pecans,
    walnuts
Oils: olive, sesame and vegetable
Olives: black and pimiento-stuffed
Pasta (dried): various shapes and sizes
Peanut butter
Pepper: black (coarse ground),
    cayenne and dried crushed red
Pickles
Preserves: apricots and grape jelly
Rice
Roasted red peppers
Salmon (canned)
Salsa
Salt
Sardines
Soy sauce
Spices: allspice, cardamom, chili
    powder, cinnamon, cloves, cumin,
    curry powder, ginger and nutmeg

than they do cooking, so you won't find fancy esoteric ingredients here. Instead, we encourage you to seek out and befriend the important people (produce, meat and dairy managers) at your local supermarket. If there is a good seafood section, make friends with them, too, or find a nearby fish market that you like.

Beyond that, we also advocate cooking in season: It makes sense when you consider that seasonal foods taste the best, cost the least and are the most readily available (which brings us back to our goal of simplifying the shopping). Besides, there is a certain sense of rightness in eating strawberries in May, corn in August and apples in October.

Once you get the hang of it, cooking with what's fresh and available is easy— and doesn't mean that you have to organize all the recipes here by season. Making dinner need not be a science, and you'll find these recipes particularly accomodating when it comes to substituting ingredients. Buy what looks good, sounds good—whatever you like. Then simply find a place for it here, in and among the more than 200 ideas for suppers you make in half an hour.

Finally, our best piece of advice is to enjoy cooking and eating with your family. It may not be everyone's best hour of the day, but that time combined with dinnertimes over the years are the stuff of togetherness and tradition.

❧

Sugar: golden brown, granulated and powdered
Tabasco sauce
Tea bags
Tomatoes: Pasta Ready diced or chunky; stewed (regular and seasoned); sun-dried
Tuna (canned): in water and olive oil
Vinegar: balsamic, cider and wine
Worcestershire sauce

## The Counter

Boboli (baked cheese pizza crust)
Bread: your favorite kind
Garlic
Onions: yellow and red
Potatoes: baking and red

## The Refrigerator

Butter
Cheese: Parmesan
Citrus fruits: orange, lemon and lime
Doughs: biscuit and pizza
Eggs
Milk: low-fat
Orange juice
Pesto sauce
Whipping cream

## The Freezer

Corn
Green peas
Frozen yogurt (or ice cream or sherbet)
Spinach (leaf)

# STOCKING THE PANTRY

Our grandmothers knew the importance of the pantry. In their day, it was a room off the kitchen where the home-canned fruits and vegetables, along with such store-bought staples as flour, sugar and coffee, were kept in the cool, dry conditions that gave rise to the term "long shelf life."

Today's pantry tends to be smaller (that extra room probably having been transformed into a home office), something along the lines of a big swing-out cupboard centrally located in the kitchen. But from our perspective, the pantry is the counter, the refrigerator and the freezer, too. Like Grandma's, it includes the basic staples that enable us to cook delicious meals every day, though Grandma wouldn't recognize many of the new products that fill our shelves.

We believe that a well-stocked pantry is the cornerstone upon which you build a repertoire of fabulous quick-cooking main courses and the side dishes to serve with them. As a result, on the list here you will find the flour, sugar and coffee of Grandma's day, along with canned cannellini beans in the cupboard and pesto sauce in the refrigerator. Those beans can be the beginnings of a warming stew in February or an innovative salad in the summer. That pesto will spruce up your favorite pizza recipe and add zip to virtually any pasta dish. We consider such convenience foods as stewed tomatoes, chicken broth and bottled marinara sauce shelf staples, pizza dough a refrigerator regular and onions the one thing no counter should be without.

## Meats and Poultry

Beef tenderloin steaks
Ground beef
Loin lamb chops
Boneless pork loin chops
Boneless chicken breast halves
Turkey breast cutlets

## Fruits and Vegetables

Apples
Bananas
Bell peppers
Broccoli
Carrots
Celery
Green onions
Lettuce
Mushrooms
Oranges
Parsley
Tomatoes

# A SUPERMARKET STRATEGY

In an ideal world, we would sit down every weekend, plan out the upcoming week and grocery shop accordingly. We would know which nights we'd feel like cooking, which evenings our husbands would be running late, which nights our kids would be busy — and so on. But while you can organize the week's meals to a degree, you can't predict every turn of events. A good solution is to keep a supply of fresh meats and poultry and some fruits and vegetables on hand in the refrigerator and freezer.

The list at left comprises what we think are the basics: those items which, when combined with the ingredients in your well-stocked pantry, guarantee that there will always be something in the house for dinner. Add to it according to what you like to eat and how you like to cook. If, for instance, you are a big pasta fan, you might add a fresh pasta to your list. If you prefer more meatless meals, you will want to include a greater variety of vegetables.

As for more perishable foods, such as fresh fish and some fruits and vegetables, knowing that you already have everything else you need on hand at home makes a quick stop for these items after work a lot more doable, even fun if you swing by a local farmers' market or a lively fishmonger's. And while you're enjoying the errand, stop in at the bakery for something really sinful for dessert.

❧

## Pots and Pans

7-inch frying pan with lid
11- or 13-inch frying pan with lid
3- quart saucepan
9 x 13-inch ovenproof glass
  baking dish
7 x 11- or 8 x 8-inch ovenproof
  glass baking dish
8-quart pot
Cast iron skillet

## Knives

8- to 10-inch chef's knife
Small paring knife
Serrated knife
Sturdy wooden chopping board

## Equipment

Coffeemaker
Food processor (full size)
Microwave oven
Toaster or toaster oven

## Utensils

Electric knife sharpener
Four-sided standing grater
Garlic press
Lemon zester
Mixing bowls
Wine opener

# EQUIPPING THE KITCHEN

A few carefully chosen pieces of kitchen equipment can make the difference between frustration and pleasure when you're cooking. The job, in other words, can be made a good deal easier with the right tool, whether it's a lemon zester or simply a sharp knife. Included here is a list of the items we couldn't do without. They help make the "30-minute kitchen" an everyday reality.

When it comes to pots and pans, you don't need cupboards full, just a couple of skillets, an all purpose saucepan, two glass baking pans and a big "pasta" pot. It's worth investing in quality skillets and saucepans, since the heavier versions conduct heat faster (always a boon) and are less likely to scorch. Ovenproof handles are a good idea, too.

Knives are another area where we recommend you invest in the best you can afford. Good knives hold an edge better and will last a long, long time.

In addition to the basics — oven, range, etc. — we like the handy items listed at left. And as for the utensils included here, these are our favorites, though it's a purely personal selection. You'll want to add to this list based on how you cook and how much you like to shop.

*—Melanie Barnard and Brooke Dojny*

# PASTA AND PIZZA

It may seem odd that two of America's favorite foods, pasta and pizza, are Italian. Actually, Italy doesn't have a sure hold on pasta either, with many food historians claiming that noodles originated in the Orient, then were transported, along with the spice trade, to us by way of Italy.

However you slice it (or twirl it), pasta and pizza are just plain delicious, which is the real reason for their popularity on both sides of the Atlantic — and the Pacific, too. They top our list of quick-cooking favorites, especially when you consider that both take less than 30 minutes to make and accommodate an unlimited number of different saucings and toppings.

Before World War II, most Americans knew very little about pasta and pizza. Returning soldiers brought with them a lingering taste for these wonderful foods, and in response, a whole new category of restaurants was born. As a country, we came to love what is now called Italian/American cooking, known for dishes like veal Parmigiana and pepperoni pizza.

Today, thanks to some very talented Italian chefs and the broadened tastes of well-traveled Americans, we know there's more to Italian food than spaghetti (good as it is). We've discovered pastas and pizzas from every region of Italy, and the other Mediterranean countries, too. We've even found that Asia has its own delicious pastas.

With all the good-quality ingredients available now, from dozens of sizes, shapes and flavors of pasta to terrific bottled marinara sauces, we could cook up a different pasta dish every night of the year. But then there would be no time to make pizza — and that just wouldn't do.

Fettuccine with Tomatoes and Prosciutto (page 15)

A long time ago we made friends with our favorite pizzeria, which sold us pizza dough by the pound so that we could make our own pizzas at home. Today we still buy that dough, but we also keep a tube of refrigerated pizza dough from the supermarket on hand to make pizzas, calzones and focaccias whenever the mood strikes (which is roughly twice a week, on average).

This chapter includes many of our favorite fast pasta recipes. Some are based on old-fashioned classics, such as Herbed Fusilli al Forno (page 19), while others are updated versions, such as Linguine with Turkey Sausage (page 41). Hot-and-Sour Thai Noodle Stir-fry (page 38) and Kung Pao Chicken with Chinese Noodles (page 24) pay homage to pasta's purported origins.

Linguine with
Turkey Sausage
(page 41)

All the pizzas here use prepared pizza dough or Bobolis, those handy baked cheese pizza crusts available in the grocery store. The toppings run the gamut from the traditional three cheeses to clams and cabbage. There's even a great barbecued chicken pizza here (page 45), a clever nod to the Americanization of that old Italian pie.

# FETTUCCINE WITH TOMATOES AND PROSCIUTTO

2 SERVINGS; CAN BE DOUBLED

All that's needed to make a meal of this fresh-tasting pasta is a radicchio salad sprinkled with Parmesan. After supper, have ripe apricots and crunchy *biscotti*. (Pictured on page 12.)

| | |
|---|---|
| 1 | pound tomatoes (about 4 medium), seeded, coarsely chopped |
| 2 | ounces sliced prosciutto, cut crosswise into ½-inch-wide strips |
| ½ | cup thinly sliced fresh basil |
| 3 | tablespoons olive oil (preferably extra-virgin) |
| 1 | tablespoon balsamic vinegar or red wine vinegar |
| 2 | large garlic cloves, minced |
| 8 | ounces fettuccine |

Mix tomatoes, prosciutto, basil, olive oil, vinegar and garlic in large bowl. Season to taste with salt and pepper.

Cook pasta in large pot of boiling salted water until tender but still firm to bite, stirring occasionally. Drain. Add pasta to tomato mixture and toss. Serve immediately.

❧

# LINGUINE TUTTOMARE

2 SERVINGS; CAN BE DOUBLED

This classic seafood pasta would be good with grilled vegetables — try onion slices and strips of zucchini and Japanese eggplant — and garlic bread. Finish up with an apricot tart.

| | |
|---|---|
| 1 | tablespoon olive oil |
| 2 | garlic cloves, minced |
| ½ | cup chopped mushrooms |
| ¼ | teaspoon cayenne pepper |
| 2 | tablespoons brandy |
| ½ | cup purchased marinara sauce |
| ½ | cup fish stock or bottled clam juice |
| 8 | mussels, scrubbed, debearded |
| 8 | clams, scrubbed |
| ⅓ | pound sea bass, cut into 1-inch pieces |
| ⅓ | pound uncooked small shrimp, peeled, deveined |
| ⅓ | pound bay scallops |
| 8 | ounces linguine |
| 2 | tablespoons chopped fresh basil |

Heat olive oil in heavy large skillet over medium-high heat. Add minced garlic; sauté 1 minute. Add chopped mushrooms and cayenne pepper; sauté 2 minutes. Add brandy and boil until all liquid evaporates, about 45 seconds. Add marinara sauce and fish stock and cook 3 minutes. Season to taste with salt and pepper. Add mussels and clams; cover and cook until shellfish open, about 6 minutes. Discard any shellfish that do not open. Add sea bass, shrimp and scallops; stir until cooked through, about 3 minutes.

Meanwhile, cook pasta in large pot of boiling salted water until just tender but still firm to the bite. Drain; transfer pasta to large bowl.

Bring sauce to simmer. Pour over pasta. Sprinkle with basil.

# Orzo with Cilantro, Shrimp and Feta

4 SERVINGS; CAN BE DOUBLED

Start the meal with a simple tomato and butter lettuce salad drizzled with lemon vinaigrette, and end it with a fruit salad of grapes and figs or oranges, adding butter cookies for crunch.
(Pictured above.)

| | |
|---|---|
| 4 | garlic cloves, peeled |
| 1 | jalapeño chili, seeded |
| 3 | cups coarsely chopped fresh cilantro |
| 1 | cup whipping cream |
| 1½ | tablespoons fresh lemon juice |
| 12 | ounces orzo (rice-shaped pasta) |
| 8 | ounces butternut squash, peeled, cut into ½-inch dice |
| 1 | pound cooked large shrimp |
| 4 | ounces feta cheese, crumbled |
| ⅓ | cup brine-cured black olives (such as Kalamata), pitted, halved |

With processor running, drop garlic and jalapeño through feed tube until finely chopped. Add cilantro and process until finely chopped. Add cream and mix using on/off turns, scraping sides of processor, until blended and thick. Add lemon juice. Season with salt and pepper.

Meanwhile, cook orzo in large pot of boiling salted water, adding diced butternut squash to pasta after 5 minutes, until pasta and squash are tender but still firm to bite. Drain. Return pasta and squash to same pot. Add cilantro mixture and toss to blend. Stir in shrimp, feta and olives, reserving some feta and a few olives for garnish. Transfer to serving bowl. Garnish with reserved olives and feta and serve.

# Pasta with Parsley and Toasted Breadcrumbs

2 SERVINGS; CAN BE DOUBLED

Make a sophisticated supper around this easy entrée by serving breadsticks and a cherry tomato salad with vinaigrette to start, and ice cream or tiramisù with espresso for the finale.

½   pound perciatelli or spaghetti

2½  tablespoons olive oil
½   cup fresh breadcrumbs made from trimmed day-old Italian bread
1   tablespoon minced garlic
⅔   cup dry white wine

1   cup packed chopped fresh parsley
⅓   cup grated Parmesan cheese (about 1 ounce)

Cook perciatelli or spaghetti in large pot of boiling salted water until just tender but still firm to bite.

Meanwhile, heat 1 tablespoon olive oil in heavy large skillet over medium-high heat. Add ½ cup breadcrumbs and stir until golden and crisp, about 2 minutes. Transfer breadcrumb mixture to plate. Reduce heat to medium. Add remaining 1½ tablespoons oil and garlic to skillet and stir 30 seconds. Add wine and simmer 2 minutes.

Drain pasta, reserving 3 tablespoons cooking water. Add pasta, reserved cooking water, parsley and cheese to skillet and toss until pasta is coated. Season to taste with salt and pepper. Sprinkle pasta with breadcrumbs and serve immediately.

# Spinach Tortellini with Three Cheeses

2 SERVINGS; CAN BE DOUBLED

To go with the tortellini, toss a salad of baby greens, oranges and sliced red onion with balsamic vinaigrette. To satisfy a sweet tooth, roll scoops of vanilla ice cream in chopped white chocolate for dessert.

2   tablespoons butter
¾   cup chopped shallots
1   teaspoon dried thyme, crumbled
½   pound mushrooms, sliced
½   cup whipping cream
2   ounces mozzarella cheese, grated
2   ounces Fontina cheese, grated
1   ounce Gorgonzola cheese, crumbled

1   9-ounce package fresh spinach cheese tortellini
   Grated Parmesan cheese (optional)

Heat butter in heavy large skillet over medium-high heat. Add shallots and thyme and sauté 2 minutes. Add mushrooms and sauté until beginning to brown and juices are released, about 6 minutes. Add cream and cook until slightly thickened. Add cheeses and stir until melted and smooth. Season to taste with pepper.

Meanwhile, cook tortellini in large pot of boiling salted water until just tender but still firm to bite. Drain. Add pasta to sauce in skillet and stir to coat. Transfer to bowl. Pass Parmesan cheese separately.

# LINGUINE WITH CRAB AND WILD MUSHROOMS

2 SERVINGS; CAN BE DOUBLED

This sophisticated main course would take well to a starter of buttered baguette rounds topped with thinly sliced smoked salmon and a sprinkling of capers. To conclude things, spoon canned apricots over toasted slices of purchased pound cake and top with a dollop of whipped cream. (Pictured at left.)

| | |
|---|---|
| 1 | 8-ounce bottle clam juice |
| ½ | teaspoon saffron threads |
| 3 | tablespoons butter |
| 7 | to 8 ounces fresh shiitake mushrooms, stemmed, sliced |
| 1 | bunch green onions, thinly sliced |
| 1 | tablespoon tomato paste |
| 8 | ounces crab meat, cut into bite-size pieces |
| 2 | teaspoons minced fresh tarragon or ¾ teaspoon dried, crumbled |
| 8 | ounces linguine pasta |

Combine clam juice and saffron threads in small bowl. Melt butter in heavy medium skillet over medium heat. Add mushrooms, sprinkle with salt and pepper and cook until beginning to soften, about 3 minutes. Add half of green onions and 1 tablespoon tomato paste and stir to blend. Add clam juice mixture and simmer 2 minutes. Add crab and tarragon and stir until heated through. Season with salt and pepper.

Meanwhile, cook linguine in large pot of boiling salted water until just tender but still firm to bite, stirring occasionally. Drain well.

Return pasta to same pot. Add sauce and toss to coat. Divide pasta between 2 plates. Sprinkle with remaining green onions and serve.

# HERBED FUSILLI AL FORNO

2 SERVINGS; CAN BE DOUBLED

A salad of sliced mushrooms, red onion and arugula makes a great beginning for this skillet-broiled pasta; coffee-flavored frozen yogurt drizzled with a little Kahlúa liqueur is a nice finale.

| | |
|---|---|
| 2 | tablespoons olive oil |
| 1 | medium zucchini, halved lengthwise, thinly sliced |
| 2 | large garlic cloves, chopped |
| 1 | 16-ounce can Italian plum tomatoes with juices |
| ½ | cup dry white wine |
| 1¼ | teaspoons dried thyme, crumbled |
| 8 | ounces fusilli or other short pasta, freshly cooked |
| 1¼ | cups packed shredded low-fat Monterey Jack cheese |

Heat olive oil in heavy medium broilerproof skillet over medium heat. Add zucchini and garlic and sauté until fragrant, about 1 minute. Add tomatoes with their juices, white wine and 1 teaspoon thyme. Bring to simmer, breaking up tomatoes with back of spoon. Cook until sauce thickens slightly and zucchini is tender, stirring occasionally, about 12 minutes. *(Can be prepared 2 hours ahead. Let stand at room temperature. Bring just to simmer before continuing.)*

Preheat broiler. Add pasta to sauce and toss to coat evenly. Sprinkle pasta with cheese. Sprinkle remaining ¼ teaspoon thyme over cheese. Broil just until cheese melts and begins to brown in spots, about 1 minute. Serve pasta immediately.

# Quick Turkey and Spinach Tetrazzini

2 SERVINGS; CAN BE DOUBLED

Complement the tetrazzini with crisp herbed flatbread and a colorful relish tray of mixed olives, radishes and carrot and celery sticks. Finish the meal with red pears and wedges of Fontina cheese.

| | |
|---|---|
| 4 | ounces spaghetti, broken into 3- to 4-inch lengths |
| 1½ | cups bite-size pieces cooked turkey |
| 1 | 9-ounce package frozen creamed spinach, thawed |
| 1 | cup part-skim ricotta cheese |
| ¼ | cup drained oil-packed sun-dried tomatoes, chopped |
| 5 | tablespoons grated Parmesan cheese |
| 1 | large garlic clove, minced |

Preheat oven to 500°F. Cook spaghetti pieces in large pot of boiling salted water until tender but still firm to bite. Drain spaghetti thoroughly, reserving ¼ cup cooking liquid.

Mix spaghetti, turkey, creamed spinach, ricotta, tomatoes, 4 tablespoons cheese, garlic and reserved cooking liquid in large bowl. Season with pepper. Spread mixture in 9-inch diameter deep-dish pie plate. Sprinkle with remaining 1 tablespoon cheese. Bake until heated through and top is light golden, about 10 minutes.

❧

# Shrimp Linguine with Pesto Cream Sauce

4 SERVINGS; CAN BE DOUBLED

Wrap thin slices of prosciutto around ripe cantaloupe slices for a great beginning to this one-dish meal, and offer mixed berries and sugar cookies for a simple dessert.

| | |
|---|---|
| ¼ | cup (½ stick) unsalted butter |
| 3 | tablespoons olive oil |
| 5 | large garlic cloves, minced |
| 1 | pound large uncooked shrimp, peeled, deveined, shells reserved |
| ½ | cup dry white wine |
| 6 | tablespoons purchased pesto sauce |
| 1½ | cups whipping cream |
| 1 | cup bottled clam juice |
| ½ | cup grated Parmesan cheese |
| | Pinch of cayenne pepper |
| 1 | pound spinach linguine, freshly cooked |
| | Additional grated Parmesan cheese |

Melt butter with oil in heavy large skillet over medium-high heat. Add garlic; stir 30 seconds. Add shrimp and sauté just until cooked through, about 3 minutes. Using slotted spoon, transfer shrimp to plate. Add reserved shrimp shells to skillet and sauté until shells turn pink, about 3 minutes. Using slotted spoon, remove shells and discard. Add wine and pesto to skillet; cook 1 minute. Add cream and clam juice and simmer until sauce is reduced to 2 cups, about 15 minutes.

Add ½ cup cheese and shrimp to sauce in skillet and simmer just until shrimp are heated through. Stir in cayenne. Season with salt and pepper. Remove from heat. Add pasta and toss to coat. Serve pasta with additional grated Parmesan cheese.

## Penne with Ham and Vegetables

2 SERVINGS; CAN BE DOUBLED

A chopped salad of mixed bitter greens like arugula, watercress and radicchio with red wine vinaigrette makes a nice first course. Finish with cookies and slices of fresh pineapple.
(Pictured above.)

| 1½ | tablespoons olive oil |
|---|---|
| 6 | ounces diced smoked ham (about 1 cup packed) |
| 1 | small red bell pepper, coarsely chopped |
| ½ | cup chopped onion |
| ½ | teaspoon dried thyme, crumbled |
| 2 | tablespoons Dijon mustard |
| ¾ | cup half and half |
| 1 | cup frozen petit peas, thawed |
| ½ | cup grated Parmesan cheese (about 1½ ounces) |
| 6 | ounces penne, freshly cooked |

Heat olive oil in heavy medium skillet over medium-high heat. Add diced ham, chopped bell pepper, chopped onion and thyme and sauté until vegetables are soft and ham begins to brown, about 6 minutes. Mix in mustard. Add half and half, peas, Parmesan cheese and pasta. Simmer until sauce reduces slightly and coats pasta, stirring occasionally, about 5 minutes. Season to taste with salt and pepper.

# CAPELLINI WITH LEMON-PARSLEY CLAM SAUCE

4 SERVINGS; CAN BE DOUBLED

Crusty bread and a curly endive and radicchio salad make excellent accompaniments to the pasta. For dessert, drizzle warm hot fudge sauce over coffee ice cream.
(Pictured below.)

3 tablespoons butter
5 tablespoons olive oil
5 large garlic cloves, chopped
2 10-ounce cans whole baby clams, drained, juices reserved
½ cup (about) bottled clam juice
⅔ cup dry white wine
1½ teaspoons dried marjoram, crumbled
¼ teaspoon dried crushed red pepper
2 tablespoons fresh lemon juice
¾ teaspoon grated lemon peel

12 ounces capellini (angel hair) or spaghettini, freshly cooked
½ cup chopped fresh parsley
Lemon wedges

Melt butter with oil in heavy large skillet over medium heat. Add garlic and sauté 1 minute. Measure reserved clam juices. Add enough bottled clam juice to equal 1½ cups. Add 1½ cups clam juice, wine, marjoram and crushed red pepper to skillet. Boil until reduced to 1¼ cups, about 7 minutes. Add clams, lemon juice and lemon peel to skillet. Simmer sauce 2 minutes.

Add pasta and all but 1 tablespoon parsley to sauce. Toss to coat pasta. Season with salt and pepper. Divide among 4 plates. Sprinkle with remaining parsley. Garnish with lemon wedges.

# PEPPERY PASTA WITH SHRIMP AND CALAMARI

2 SERVINGS; CAN BE DOUBLED

This spicy seafood pasta makes a satisfying supper. For a colorful salad alongside, marinate steamed broccoli, cauliflower and roasted red bell peppers (the kind packed in a jar is fine) in Italian dressing. Dessert might be slices of cheesecake topped with seasonal fruits.

| | |
|---|---|
| 8 | ounces fusilli or other corkscrew pasta |
| 1 | 14½-ounce can "Pasta Ready" chunky tomatoes |
| ½ | cup dry red wine |
| ¼ | teaspoon dried crushed red pepper |
| 4 | ounces cleaned calamari, bodies cut crosswise into rings |
| 4 | ounces uncooked shrimp, peeled, deveined |
| ½ | cup chopped Italian parsley |

Grated Parmesan cheese

Cook fusilli pasta in medium pot of boiling salted water until just tender but still firm to bite.

Meanwhile, simmer tomatoes with their juices, wine and crushed red pepper in heavy medium saucepan over medium heat until mixture begins to thicken, about 5 minutes. Add calamari, shrimp and parsley and simmer until seafood is just cooked through, 3 minutes.

Drain pasta and add to sauce. Toss until pasta is lightly coated. Season to taste with salt and pepper. Serve, passing cheese separately.

❧

# TOMATO-ANCHOVY PASTA

2 GENEROUS SERVINGS; CAN BE DOUBLED

To make a meal of this Sicilian-style pasta, precede it with bowls of minestrone soup, add crusty Italian bread, and end on a citrusy note: sliced oranges and chocolate-dipped *biscotti*.

| | |
|---|---|
| ¼ | cup olive oil |
| 1 | cup chopped green onions (about 5) |
| 4 | garlic cloves, minced |
| 1 | 2-ounce can anchovy fillets, drained, chopped |
| 1 | 14½- to 16-ounce can diced peeled tomatoes |
| ¾ | pound rotini or other corkscrew-shaped pasta |
| ½ | cup grated Parmesan cheese |

Heat olive oil in heavy large skillet over medium-high heat. Add green onions and garlic and sauté until soft, about 5 minutes. Add anchovies and stir 1 minute. Add canned tomatoes and simmer until sauce thickens slightly, about 6 minutes. *(Can be prepared 2 hours ahead. Let sauce stand at room temperature.)*

Cook rotini in large pot of boiling salted water until just tender but still firm to bite. Drain, reserving ½ cup cooking liquid. Add reserved cooking liquid to tomato-anchovy sauce in skillet and stir over medium-high heat until heated through. Add rotini and toss until sauce coats rotini. Add Parmesan cheese and toss to blend. Season pasta to taste with salt and pepper and serve.

# KUNG PAO CHICKEN WITH CHINESE NOODLES

4 SERVINGS; CAN BE DOUBLED

Instead of serving the chicken with rice, as is traditional, it's tossed with fresh Chinese noodles, which you can find in the refrigerated Asian section of most supermarkets. Get things going with purchased egg rolls, and for a cool and refreshing conclusion to the meal, offer orange sorbet with fortune cookies. (Pictured at right.)

⅓ cup canned low-salt chicken broth
⅓ cup low-sodium soy sauce
⅓ cup dry sherry
2 tablespoons cornstarch
2 skinless boneless chicken breast halves, cut into strips
1 12-ounce package fresh water noodles or linguine

1½ tablespoons oriental sesame oil
2 teaspoons minced garlic
2 teaspoons minced peeled fresh ginger
½ teaspoon dried crushed red pepper
2 cups snow peas, trimmed
6 green onions, cut into 1-inch pieces
½ cup roasted unsalted peanuts

Combine chicken broth, soy sauce, sherry and 1 tablespoon cornstarch in small bowl. Toss chicken with remaining 1 tablespoon cornstarch. Cook noodles in large pot of boiling salted water until just tender but still firm to bite, about 5 minutes. Drain.

Heat oil in heavy large skillet or wok over high heat. Add garlic, ginger and crushed red pepper and stir 30 seconds. Add chicken and sauté 2 minutes. Transfer chicken to plate. Add snow peas and green onions to skillet and sauté 1 minute. Return chicken to skillet; add peanuts and chicken broth mixture and cook until mixture thickens slightly, about 1 minute. Add noodles to skillet and toss to coat. Serve.

# THAI SHRIMP AND ARTICHOKE PASTA

4 SERVINGS; CAN BE DOUBLED

You can add chopped roasted peanuts as a garnish for this lively salad. To go with it, cook up some frozen dim sum dumplings and serve with a mustard-soy dipping sauce. Buy Thai iced tea for a deliciously authentic beverage. (By the way, if chili-sesame oil isn't available, substitute oriental sesame oil mixed with dried crushed red pepper.)

¾ cup rice vinegar
2 tablespoons chili-sesame oil
2 tablespoons soy sauce
1½ tablespoons chopped peeled fresh ginger
1 tablespoon Dijon mustard

1 12-ounce package fresh water noodles or linguine pasta, freshly cooked
¾ pound peeled cooked shrimp
2 6-ounce jars marinated artichoke hearts, drained
1 cup chopped green onions
¼ cup chopped fresh cilantro
¼ cup chopped fresh mint

Combine first 5 ingredients in blender and puree. Season dressing with salt and pepper *(Can be prepared 1 day ahead. Cover and chill.)*

Combine remaining ingredients in bowl. Toss with enough dressing to coat. Pass extra dressing separately.

## RIGATONI WITH TOMATOES AND VODKA

4 SERVINGS; CAN BE DOUBLED

Head for the nearest deli, where you can buy all the fixings for a mini-antipasto to go with this pasta: caponata (that delicious eggplant salad/relish), marinated mushrooms, cheeses and brine-cured olives. Pick up cannoli for dessert, while you're there.
(Pictured above.)

| | |
|---|---|
| 2 | tablespoons (¼ stick) butter |
| 1 | small onion, chopped |
| 2 | garlic cloves, minced |
| 1 | tablespoon dried Italian seasonings, crumbled |
| 1 | 16-ounce can Italian plum tomatoes, chopped, juices reserved |
| 3 | ounces sliced prosciutto or ham, chopped |
| ½ | cup vodka |
| ¾ | cup whipping cream |
| 1 | cup grated Parmesan cheese |
| 8 | ounces rigatoni or other tubular pasta, freshly cooked |

Melt butter in heavy large skillet over medium-high heat. Add onion, garlic and Italian seasonings and sauté until onion is translucent, about 4 minutes. Add tomatoes, reserved juices and prosciutto and simmer 10 minutes, stirring occasionally. Add vodka and simmer 5 minutes. Add cream and ½ cup Parmesan. Simmer until sauce thickens slightly, about 4 minutes. Add rigatoni and stir until sauce coats pasta. Season with salt and pepper. Serve pasta immediately, passing remaining ½ cup Parmesan cheese separately.

# SEASHELL PASTA WITH SALMON AND FRESH DILL

2 SERVINGS; CAN BE DOUBLED

Canned salmon would make this main course even quicker. Arrange colorful cucumber slices around the pasta, and accompany with fresh crisp breadsticks. Lemonade is a nice change from wine or iced tea. Purchased blueberry turnovers would round out this menu.

| | |
|---|---|
| l | 8-ounce ¾-inch-thick salmon fillet with skin |
| | Olive oil |
| 4 | ounces small pasta shells |
| ½ | cup chopped red onion |
| ½ | cup chopped celery |
| ⅓ | cup regular or reduced-calorie mayonnaise |
| 3 | tablespoons chopped fresh dill |
| l | tablespoon country-style Dijon mustard |
| | Fresh dill sprigs |

Preheat broiler. Brush both sides of salmon with oil. Season with salt and pepper. Broil salmon until just cooked through, about 3 minutes per side. Cool salmon slightly.

Meanwhile, cook pasta in large pot of boiling salted water until tender but still firm to bite. Drain. Rinse with cold water and drain again. Transfer to bowl. Add onion and celery. Skin salmon and break into pieces. Add salmon to pasta mixture.

Whisk mayonnaise, chopped dill and mustard to blend in small bowl. Add to pasta and toss. *(Can be prepared 6 hours ahead. Cover and chill).* Divide pasta between 2 plates. Garnish with dill and serve.

# TORTELLINI WITH BROCCOLI AND RED PEPPER

2 SERVINGS; CAN BE DOUBLED

Mix artichoke hearts, romaine lettuce and garlic croutons then toss with Caesar dressing for a salad to go with the pasta. Dessert might be a superfast peach melba: Place a scoop of vanilla ice cream on a peach half and top with raspberries. (If you double this recipe, boil the wine-vinegar mixture one minute.)

| | |
|---|---|
| 9 | ounces fresh or frozen cheese tortellini |
| 4 | tablespoons olive oil |
| 2½ | cups (about 5 ounces) broccoli florets |
| l | red bell pepper, thinly sliced |
| l | large garlic clove, minced |
| ⅓ | cup dry white wine |
| l | teaspoon white wine vinegar |
| | Grated Parmesan cheese |

Cook tortellini in large pot of boiling salted water according to package directions. Drain thoroughly.

Meanwhile, heat olive oil in heavy large skillet over medium-high heat. Add broccoli florets and sliced red bell pepper to skillet and sauté until vegetables are tender, about 3 minutes. Add garlic and stir 1 minute. Add wine and vinegar to skillet and cook 30 seconds. Add cooked tortellini and toss until heated through, about 1 minute. Season pasta to taste with salt and pepper. Divide tortellini mixture between two plates and serve, passing Parmesan cheese separately.

# Tuna Pasta Verde

2 SERVINGS; CAN BE DOUBLED

This is our contemporary version of tuna-noodle casserole, the well-loved dish from the 1950s. Try serving it with a green salad and crisp Italian breadsticks; follow the meal with lemon sorbet.

| | |
|---|---|
| 1 | 6⅛-ounce can solid white oil-packed tuna, drained, broken into chunks, 1 tablespoon oil reserved |
| 1 | red bell pepper, thinly sliced |
| 2 | garlic cloves, minced |
| 1¼ | cups half and half |
| ½ | cup canned chicken broth |
| ¼ | cup chopped fresh basil or 1½ teaspoons dried, crumbled |
| 6 | ounces spinach fettuccine, freshly cooked |
| 6 | tablespoons grated Parmesan cheese |
| 2 | tablespoons plain dried breadcrumbs |

Preheat broiler. Heat 1 tablespoon reserved tuna oil in heavy medium broilerproof skillet over medium-high heat. Add red pepper and garlic and sauté mixture 1 minute. Add half and half, broth and basil and simmer until mixture is reduced to 1 cup, about 8 minutes. Add pasta, 4 tablespoons Parmesan and tuna. Toss gently. Sprinkle remaining 2 tablespoons Parmesan and breadcrumbs over top. Broil until topping is brown, about 1 minute.

# Greek-Style Penne

4 SERVINGS; CAN BE DOUBLED

Stuffed grape leaves from a Mediterranean deli along with lemon wedges and plain yogurt would be a nice starter here, while baklava, which you can often buy in delis by the piece, would be the ideal ending.

| | |
|---|---|
| 8 | bacon slices, chopped |
| 1 | large onion, chopped |
| 1 | small eggplant, cut into 1-inch cubes |
| 2 | cups chopped seeded tomatoes |
| 4 | large garlic cloves, chopped |
| 1 | tablespoon red wine vinegar |
| 1 | teaspoon dried thyme, crumbled |
| ⅓ | cup drained capers, rinsed |
| 1 | pound penne pasta |
| 2 | tablespoons olive oil |
| 1½ | cups feta cheese (about 7 ounces), crumbled |
| ½ | cup pitted, brine-cured black olives (such as Kalamata) |
| | Chopped Italian parsley |

Cook bacon in heavy large skillet over medium-high heat until crisp. Transfer to paper towels using slotted spoon. Add onion and eggplant to drippings in skillet. Sauté over medium-high heat until eggplant is tender and golden, about 15 minutes. Add tomatoes, garlic, vinegar and thyme. Reduce heat to medium and cook 5 minutes. Stir in capers. Season to taste with salt and pepper.

Cook pasta in large pot of boiling salted water until just tender but still firm to bite. Drain. Transfer to large bowl. Toss with olive oil. Mix in eggplant sauce, feta, olives and bacon. Sprinkle with parsley.

# SHRIMP AND FRESH HERB LINGUINE

4 SERVINGS; CAN BE DOUBLED

Accompany the pasta with a romaine and tomato salad and hot Italian bread. Fresh ripe peaches splashed with Champagne make a great dessert. (Pictured below.)

| | |
|---|---|
| 12 | ounces linguine |
| 7 | tablespoons unsalted butter |
| 3 | tablespoons olive oil |
| 1 | pound medium uncooked shrimp, peeled, deveined |
| 8 | garlic cloves, minced |
| 1/3 | cup chopped shallots |
| 2/3 | cup bottled clam juice |
| 1/2 | cup dry white wine |
| 1/2 | cup chopped fresh parsley |
| 1/4 | cup chopped fresh dill or 1 tablespoon dried dillweed |
| 1 | teaspoon pepper |

Cook linguine in large pot of boiling salted water until just tender but still firm to bite, stirring occasionally. Drain pasta and return to same pot to keep warm. Mix in 1 tablespoon butter.

Meanwhile, heat oil in heavy large skillet over medium heat. Add shrimp and sauté until just cooked through, stirring frequently, about 3 minutes. Using slotted spoon, transfer shrimp to bowl. Add garlic, shallots and 1 tablespoon butter to skillet. Cook 2 minutes. Add clam juice and wine. Increase heat and boil until mixture is reduced by half, about 8 minutes. Whisk in remaining 5 tablespoons butter. Return shrimp and any accumulated juices to skillet. Add parsley, dill, pepper and pasta and toss to blend well. Season to taste with salt.

# PASTA SALAD WITH GRILLED VEGETABLES

2 SERVINGS; CAN BE DOUBLED

Add some sesame breadsticks, and you've got a satisfying meatless entrée. Finish with tiramisù from the bakery and cups of steaming espresso. (Pictured at left.)

6 ounces penne pasta
6 tablespoons bottled Italian dressing with olive oil

2 medium Japanese eggplants, cut in half lengthwise
1 large red bell pepper, quartered
1 medium zucchini, cut in half lengthwise
1 cup crumbled feta cheese (about 4 ounces)
⅓ cup slivered fresh basil leaves

Prepare barbecue (medium-high heat). Cook pasta in large pot of boiling salted water until tender but still firm to bite. Drain pasta. Place in large bowl and toss with 3 tablespoons dressing.

Meanwhile, grill eggplants, red bell pepper and zucchini until tender and slightly charred, brushing with remaining 3 tablespoons dressing and turning occasionally, about 5 minutes. Cut vegetables into 1-inch pieces. Add to pasta with cheese and basil and toss to combine. Season to taste with salt and pepper.

# MEDITERRANEAN SEASHELL PASTA

4 SERVINGS; CAN BE DOUBLED

This lovely pasta doesn't need much in the way of accompaniments, but you could begin the meal with toasted baguette slices topped with a mixture of chopped tomatoes, black brine-cured olives and basil in balsamic vinaigrette. Later, offer slices of chocolate-raspberry tart from the bakery.

2 tablespoons olive oil
1 large fennel bulb, coarsely chopped
1 large onion, coarsely chopped
4 large garlic cloves, minced
1 28-ounce can crushed tomatoes with puree
⅔ cup chopped oil-packed sun-dried tomatoes
½ cup black brine-cured olives (such as Kalamata), pitted, halved
2 teaspoons chopped fresh rosemary or ¾ teaspoon dried, crumbled

12 ounces shell pasta
Grated Parmesan cheese

Heat oil in heavy large skillet over medium-high heat. Add fennel, onion and garlic and sauté until almost tender, about 9 minutes. Add crushed tomatoes with puree, sun-dried tomatoes, olives and rosemary and simmer just until slightly thickened, about 3 minutes. Season sauce to taste with salt and pepper.

Meanwhile, cook pasta in large pot of boiling salted water until just tender but still firm to bite. Drain. Add pasta to skillet with sauce and toss to coat. Transfer to large bowl; sprinkle with Parmesan.

# SPAGHETTINI TONNATO

2 SERVINGS; CAN BE DOUBLED

Fresh tuna stars in this Mediterranean pasta sauce. Don't forget the Italian bread to soak up the juices. End with sliced fruit drizzled with Sambuca, an anise-flavored liqueur from Italy. (Pictured below.)

| | |
|---|---|
| 3 | tablespoons olive oil |
| 1 | 8- to 10-ounce 1-inch-thick fresh tuna steak |
| 3 | large garlic cloves, minced |
| 1 | anchovy fillet, chopped |
| 1 | 16-ounce can Italian tomatoes with juices |
| ¼ | cup chopped pitted brine-cured olives (such as Kalamata) |
| ¼ | cup chopped fresh Italian parsley |
| 6 | ounces spaghettini or thin spaghetti, freshly cooked |

Heat 1 tablespoon oil in heavy medium skillet over medium-high heat. Season tuna with salt and pepper. Add tuna to skillet and sear until almost cooked through, about 3 minutes per side. Transfer tuna to plate. Reduce heat to medium. Add remaining 2 tablespoons oil, garlic and anchovy to skillet and sauté until fragrant, about 1 minute. Add tomatoes and cook until reduced to sauce consistency, breaking up tomatoes with back of spoon, about 12 minutes.

Add olives and parsley to sauce and simmer 1 minute. Cut tuna into ¾-inch pieces and add to sauce with any accumulated juices. Simmer until tuna is just cooked through, stirring frequently, about 1 minute. Season sauce with salt and pepper. Spoon over pasta.

# PASTA WITH CHICKEN AND CHEESE

4 SERVINGS; CAN BE DOUBLED

Make an elegant and easy first course by cooking frozen artichoke hearts and serving them with some garlicky mayonnaise. Cream puffs from the bakery would make an irresistibly indulgent dessert.

¼ cup olive oil
3 large boneless chicken breast halves, cut into 1-inch cubes
1 onion, chopped
1 garlic clove, chopped
½ teaspoon fennel seeds
1 carrot, peeled, cut into matchstick-size strips
¼ cup finely chopped drained oil-packed sun-dried tomatoes
12 ounces fettuccine, freshly cooked
1 cup grated Parmesan cheese

Heat oil in heavy large skillet over medium-high heat. Add chicken and sauté until brown and cooked through, about 6 minutes. Using slotted spoon, transfer chicken to large bowl. Keep warm.

Add onion, garlic and fennel seeds to skillet and sauté until onion is tender, about 6 minutes. Stir in carrot and sun-dried tomatoes and continue cooking until carrot is crisp-tender, stirring occasionally, about 2 minutes. Transfer mixture to bowl with chicken. Add pasta and Parmesan and toss well. Serve immediately.

# SUN-DRIED TOMATO FETTUCCINE

4 SERVINGS; CAN BE DOUBLED

For a quick pizza hors d'oeuvre, top a small Boboli crust with pesto, goat cheese and strips of roasted bell pepper from a jar; bake until crisp, and then cut into wedges. Dessert might be as simple as coffee ice cream sprinkled with grated chocolate and cookie crumbs.

1 cup dry-pack sun-dried tomatoes
½ cup olive oil
4 garlic cloves, minced
½ teaspoon dried crushed red pepper
1 pound fettuccine, freshly cooked
1 cup grated Parmesan cheese
½ cup toasted pine nuts
Additional grated Parmesan cheese

Place sun-dried tomatoes in small bowl. Add enough boiling water to just cover tomatoes. Let stand until tomatoes are soft, about 1 minute. Drain. Coarsely chop tomatoes.

Heat olive oil in heavy small skillet. Add sun-dried tomatoes, garlic and dried crushed red pepper. Sauté until garlic is just golden, about 3 minutes. Transfer mixture to large bowl. Add fettuccine and 1 cup Parmesan. Toss well. Sprinkle with pine nuts. Serve immediately, passing additional Parmesan cheese separately.

## MIXED MUSHROOM PASTA

2 SERVINGS; CAN BE DOUBLED

Make a salad to go with the pasta by sprinkling imported olives over sliced oranges and red onions and drizzling with a red wine vinaigrette. Spumoni ice cream and cups of espresso wrap up the meal in Italian style.
(Pictured at right.)

6    ounces fettuccine
1    tablespoon butter
8    ounces mixed fresh button and wild mushrooms, thinly sliced
1    large garlic clove, chopped
½    teaspoon dried tarragon, crumbled
½    cup whipping cream
1½   tablespoons Madeira
     Chopped fresh parsley

Cook pasta in large pot of boiling salted water until just tender but still firm to bite. Drain thoroughly.

Meanwhile, melt butter in heavy medium skillet over medium-low heat. Add mushrooms and garlic; sauté until beginning to soften, about 5 minutes. Add tarragon and sauté until mushrooms begin to release some juices, about 2 minutes. Add whipping cream and Madeira; simmer just to blend, about 1 minute. Add pasta to sauce; toss to coat. Season with salt and pepper. Garnish with parsley and serve.

## PERCIATELLI WITH TUNA, CAPERS AND TOMATOES

2 SERVINGS; CAN BE DOUBLED

Country-style Italian bread and a hearty salad of romaine with roasted peppers and black olives would be great with this pasta dish. Fresh pears with walnuts and Gorgonzola are an appropriate dessert.

8    ounces perciatelli or spaghetti
2    tablespoons olive oil
4    rolled fillets of anchovies with capers from can
3    garlic cloves, minced
1    14½-ounce can "Pasta Ready" chunky tomatoes
¼    cup dry white wine
1    6⅛-ounce can white tuna packed in water, drained well
3    tablespoons chopped parsley

Cook perciatelli pasta in large pot of boiling salted water until just tender but still firm to bite.

Meanwhile, heat oil in heavy large skillet over medium-low heat. Add anchovies with capers and garlic and sauté 2 minutes, mashing to paste with back of fork. Mix in tomatoes with their juices and wine. Increase heat to medium-high and simmer until sauce thickens slightly, about 5 minutes. Add tuna and parsley and mix to break up large tuna chunks. Drain pasta. Add to sauce and toss to blend. Season to taste with pepper and serve.

# FETTUCCINE WITH SPINACH-RICOTTA SAUCE

4 SERVINGS; CAN BE DOUBLED

Serve this colorful pasta with crisp breadsticks and thinly sliced red and yellow bell peppers drizzled with olive oil and red wine vinegar. For dessert, offer fresh strawberries.
(Pictured below.)

| | |
|---|---|
| 3 | tablespoons olive oil |
| 1 | medium onion, chopped |
| 3 | large garlic cloves, minced |
| 1 | tablespoon all purpose flour |
| 2 | cups milk (do not use lowfat or nonfat) |
| 1 | 10-ounce package frozen chopped spinach, thawed, well drained |
| 1 | cup ricotta cheese |
| 1/3 | cup grated Parmesan cheese |
| 10 | oil-packed sun-dried tomatoes, drained, cut into thin strips |
| 3 | tablespoons chopped fresh basil or 2 teaspoons dried, crumbled |
| 1/4 | teaspoon ground nutmeg |
| 1 | pound fettuccine, freshly cooked |
| 1/3 | cup minced green onions |
| 1/3 | cup toasted pine nuts |
| | Grated Parmesan cheese |

Heat oil in heavy medium saucepan over medium heat. Add onion and cook until translucent, stirring occasionally, about 4 minutes. Add garlic and cook 1 minute. Stir in flour and cook 1 minute. Gradually whisk in milk and cook until sauce is smooth and bubbling, stirring, about 4 minutes. Mix in spinach, ricotta, 1/3 cup Parmesan, tomatoes, basil and nutmeg. Season with salt and pepper. Simmer over medium-low heat until heated through, 5 minutes.

Transfer pasta to platter. Spoon sauce over. Garnish with onions and pine nuts. Sprinkle with pepper. Serve, passing Parmesan.

# Gnocchi with Broccoli and Garbanzo Beans

2 SERVINGS; CAN BE DOUBLED

To start this meal right, prepare an easy-to-assemble platter of purchased caponata (eggplant relish), Italian olives, roasted peppers and seeded breadsticks. Finish up dinner by drizzling sliced oranges with Grand Marnier.

| | |
|---|---|
| 2 | tablespoons olive oil |
| 1 | tablespoon minced garlic |
| ⅔ | cup dry white wine |
| 1 | 15-ounce can garbanzo beans (chick-peas), rinsed, drained |
| | Pinch of dried crushed red pepper |
| 6 | ounces gnocchi pasta or small shell pasta |
| 3 | cups broccoli florets (from about 2 large stalks) |
| ½ | cup grated Parmesan cheese |

Heat oil in heavy large skillet over medium-high heat. Add garlic; sauté 1 minute. Add wine, garbanzo beans and crushed red pepper; cook until sauce thickens slightly, about 5 minutes.

Meanwhile, cook pasta in medium pot of boiling salted water until almost tender, about 8 minutes. Add broccoli and cook until broccoli is crisp-tender and pasta is tender but still firm to bite, about 3 minutes longer. Drain pasta thoroughly.

Add pasta, broccoli and cheese to sauce in skillet and toss until coated. Season to taste with salt and pepper.

# Penne with Mushrooms and Gorgonzola

2 GENEROUS SERVINGS; CAN BE DOUBLED

For an instant appetizer, toss lightly steamed yellow wax beans and sliced roasted red peppers with balsamic vinegar and Parmesan cheese. After the rich pasta, scoops of fruit sorbet and cookies would be refreshing.

| | |
|---|---|
| ¼ | cup olive oil |
| 3 | large garlic cloves, chopped |
| ½ | pound mushrooms, sliced |
| 4 | plum tomatoes, chopped |
| 2 | tablespoons chopped fresh basil or 2 teaspoons dried, crumbled |
| 2 | tablespoons chopped fresh oregano or 2 teaspoons dried, crumbled |
| ¾ | pound penne or other tubular pasta |
| ½ | cup crumbled Gorgonzola cheese or other blue cheese |

Heat olive oil in heavy large skillet over medium-high heat. Add garlic; sauté 1 minute. Add mushrooms; sauté until beginning to soften, about 5 minutes. Add tomatoes, basil and oregano and simmer until sauce thickens slightly, about 5 minutes. *(Can be prepared 2 hours ahead. Let sauce stand at room temperature.)*

Cook penne in large pot of boiling salted water until just tender but still firm to bite. Drain, reserving ½ cup cooking liquid. Add pasta and cooking liquid to sauce in skillet. Toss over medium heat until mixture is heated through and sauce coats pasta. Season with salt and pepper. Transfer pasta to bowl. Sprinkle with Gorgonzola and serve.

## CREAMY FETTUCCINE WITH BACON

4 SERVINGS; CAN BE DOUBLED

This rich and creamy pasta is perfectly balanced by a crisp salad of mixed baby greens tossed with a lemon vinaigrette. For dessert, try slices of fresh pineapple with butter cookies.

8   ounces bacon, chopped
1   cup shredded carrots
1   cup frozen peas, thawed
1   cup chopped fresh parsley
2   cups whipping cream
2   cups grated Parmesan cheese
1   pound fettuccine, freshly cooked

Cook bacon in heavy large skillet over medium-high heat until crisp. Using slotted spoon, transfer bacon to paper towel to drain. Pour off all but 1 tablespoon fat from skillet. Add carrots, peas and parsley and sauté 1 minute. Mix in cream and Parmesan and simmer until sauce thickens slightly, about 3 minutes. Season to taste with salt and pepper. Place fettuccine in large bowl. Add cream mixture and toss well. Sprinkle with cooked bacon and serve.

## HOT-AND-SOUR THAI NOODLE STIR-FRY

4 SERVINGS; CAN BE DOUBLED

In this vegetarian entrée, thin noodles are tossed with tofu, colorful vegetables and a wonderfully spicy Thai-style peanut and lime sauce. Start the meal off by serving vegetable broth with chopped green onion tops. For dessert, try coconut ice cream or a fruit sorbet.

3    garlic cloves
⅔    cup creamy peanut butter (do not use old-fashioned style or freshly ground)
3    tablespoons fresh lime juice
3    tablespoons soy sauce
½    teaspoon dried crushed red pepper
½    cup vegetable broth

10   ounces dried Japanese-style noodles (udon) or linguine
8    ounces snow peas, halved

3    tablespoons vegetable oil
2    red bell peppers, thinly sliced
14   ounces firm tofu, cubed, drained well on paper towels

2    green onions, sliced
3    tablespoons chopped fresh cilantro

Finely chop garlic in processor. Scrape down sides of work bowl. Add peanut butter, lime juice, soy sauce and crushed red pepper. Process to blend ingredients. With machine running, slowly pour vegetable broth through feed tube and process until sauce is smooth.

Cook noodles in boiling salted water until just tender but still firm to bite. Add snow peas during last 30 seconds. Drain.

Meanwhile, heat oil in wok or heavy large skillet over high heat. Add bell peppers and stir-fry until just tender, about 2 minutes. Remove with slotted spoon. Add tofu and stir-fry until just beginning to brown, about 1 minute. Return bell peppers to skillet and stir until hot.

Remove skillet from heat. Add noodles, peas and peanut sauce. Mix to coat noodles and vegetables evenly. Transfer noodle mixture to platter. Garnish with green onions and cilantro and serve.

# Linguine with Chicken, Leeks and Tomatoes

4 SERVINGS; CAN BE DOUBLED

For a satisfying first course, pass a platter of Italian cold cuts and cheeses, pickled vegetables and focaccia (that terrific flat, herbed bread). Buy ricotta cheese tartlets for dessert. (Pictured below.)

| | |
|---|---|
| 2 | tablespoons olive oil |
| 4 | skinless boneless chicken breast halves |
| ¼ | cup (½ stick) butter |
| 3 | large leeks (white and pale green parts only), thinly sliced or 1 large onion, chopped |
| 4 | garlic cloves, minced |
| 1 | 28-ounce can Italian plum tomatoes, drained, chopped |
| 2 | tablespoons dry vermouth |
| 1 | pound linguine, freshly cooked |
| 1 | cup grated Parmesan cheese |
| ¼ | cup chopped fresh basil (optional) |

Heat olive oil in heavy large skillet over medium-high heat. Season chicken with salt and pepper. Add to skillet and sauté until just cooked through, about 3 minutes per side. Cool chicken slightly. Thinly slice chicken crosswise and set aside.

Melt butter in same skillet over medium-low heat. Add leeks and garlic and sauté until leeks are very tender, about 10 minutes. Stir in tomatoes, vermouth and chicken. Cook until mixture is just heated through, about 2 minutes. Season generously with salt and pepper. Combine chicken mixture, linguine and ½ cup Parmesan in large bowl; toss well. Sprinkle with basil. Serve, passing remaining Parmesan.

# LINGUINE WITH TURKEY SAUSAGE

4 SERVINGS; CAN BE DOUBLED

For openers, try a spinach salad with red wine vinaigrette and slices of toasted sourdough bread. Serve scoops of lemon sherbet after dinner. (Pictured at left.)

| | |
|---|---|
| 2 | tablespoons olive oil |
| ¾ | pound fully cooked turkey sausage (such as kielbasa), cut into ½-inch pieces |
| 1 | red bell pepper, diced |
| 6 | large mushrooms (about 6 ounces), sliced |
| 4 | green onions, thinly sliced |
| ¾ | pound linguine, freshly cooked |
| ½ | cup purchased pesto sauce |
| ½ | cup grated Parmesan cheese |
| | Additional grated Parmesan cheese |

Heat olive oil in heavy large skillet over medium-high heat. Add sausage, bell pepper, mushrooms and green onions. Sauté mixture until vegetables soften, about 7 minutes. Add pasta, pesto sauce and ½ cup Parmesan. Toss until mixture is combined. Season to taste with salt and pepper. Serve immediately, passing additional Parmesan separately.

# ANGEL HAIR FRITTATA

4 SERVINGS; CAN BE DOUBLED

This Italian-inspired main course needs only warm sourdough rolls to complete it. For dessert, whip up a fresh fruit salad and sprinkle it with a little crème de cassis for added flavor.

| | |
|---|---|
| 4 | tablespoons olive oil |
| 2 | small zucchini, sliced |
| 1 | tomato, seeded, chopped |
| 2 | large mushrooms, sliced |
| 1 | green onion, sliced |
| 4 | garlic cloves, minced |
| 2 | tablespoons chopped black olives |
| ¼ | teaspoon dried basil, crumbled |
| ⅛ | teaspoon dried oregano, crumbled |
| | |
| 4 | eggs |
| 1½ | cups grated Romano cheese |
| 6 | ounces angel hair pasta, freshly cooked |
| | Additional grated Romano cheese |
| 2 | tomatoes, chopped |

Heat 2 tablespoons oil in heavy medium skillet over medium-high heat. Add zucchini, 1 tomato, mushrooms, onion and garlic and sauté until tender, about 3 minutes. Add olives and herbs. Cool.

Preheat broiler. Beat eggs and 1½ cups cheese in large bowl. Season with salt and pepper. Mix in vegetables and pasta. Heat remaining 2 tablespoons oil in heavy large broilerproof skillet over medium heat. Add egg mixture to skillet. Press mixture with back of spatula to even thickness. Cook until frittata is set and golden brown on bottom. Transfer skillet to broiler and cook until top of frittata is set, about 2 minutes. Run small knife around edge of frittata to loosen. Invert skillet onto large plate. Remove skillet. Cut frittata into wedges. Serve, passing additional cheese and chopped tomatoes separately.

# BACON, CABBAGE AND GRUYÈRE PIZZA

4 SERVINGS; CAN BE DOUBLED

One of our favorite convenience products — packaged pizza crust — is put to excellent use in this recipe, which transforms readily available ingredients into a fast and easy main course. Begin with canned bean soup jazzed up with chopped tomatoes and herbs. Pour cream over baked pears for dessert.

8    slices bacon, diced
½    small head green cabbage, thinly sliced
1    tablespoon caraway seeds
1    teaspoon cider vinegar

1    16-ounce baked cheese pizza crust (such as Boboli)
2    tablespoons Dijon mustard
¾    cup packed grated Gruyère cheese
¾    cup packed grated mozzarella cheese

Preheat oven to 400°F. Sauté bacon in heavy large skillet over medium heat until brown and crisp. Using slotted spoon, transfer bacon to paper towels and drain. Pour off drippings from skillet and discard. Add cabbage to same skillet and sauté until wilted, about 5 minutes. Sprinkle caraway seeds and vinegar over and blend well. Season cabbage mixture with salt and pepper.

Place pizza crust on heavy large baking sheet. Spread with mustard, then cabbage mixture. Sprinkle with bacon. Top with cheeses, spreading evenly. Bake until cheese melts and crust is crisp, 20 minutes.

# EGGPLANT AND TOMATO PIZZA

2 SERVINGS; CAN BE DOUBLED

All you need to complete this easy meal is a tossed green salad. For a clever dessert, dip small squares of purchased pound cake in melted chocolate and refrigerate until firm.

2    tablespoons olive oil
2    cups ½-inch cubes unpeeled Japanese eggplant (about 8 ounces)
1    medium onion, thinly sliced

1    10-ounce tube refrigerated pizza dough
8    ounces plum tomatoes, thinly sliced
3    tablespoons grated Parmesan cheese
¾    teaspoon dried marjoram, crumbled

Preheat oven to 450°F. Lightly oil 9 x 9 x 2-inch baking pan. Heat oil in heavy medium skillet over medium-high heat. Add eggplant and onion and sauté until vegetables soften and brown lightly, about 10 minutes. Season to taste with salt and pepper.

Unroll pizza dough. Fit into prepared pan, pressing up at edges to create 1-inch-high rim. Spread eggplant mixture evenly over bottom of crust. Arrange tomatoes over. Sprinkle with cheese and marjoram.

Bake until topping is heated through and edges of pizza are brown and crisp, about 15 minutes. Cut into squares and serve.

# FRENCH BREAD PIZZA WITH SAUSAGE AND MUSHROOMS

6 SERVINGS; CAN BE DOUBLED

These pizza "sandwiches" would go well with a side dish of sautéed zucchini, red bell pepper and crookneck squash. Chocolate cupcakes will please the younger and older sets alike. (Pictured above.)

| | |
|---|---|
| 1 | pound sweet Italian sausage, casings removed |
| 1 | pound mushrooms, sliced |
| 2 | large garlic cloves, minced |
| 1 | teaspoon dried oregano, crumbled |
| 1 | 1-pound loaf French bread, cut in half lengthwise |
| | Olive oil |
| 1 | 15-ounce container marinara sauce |
| 16 | ounces shredded mozzarella cheese |
| ½ | cup grated Parmesan cheese |

Cook sausage in heavy large skillet over medium-high heat, breaking up sausage with fork until cooked through, about 7 minutes. Using slotted spoon transfer sausage to plate. Pour off all but 2 tablespoons fat from skillet. Add mushrooms, garlic and oregano to skillet and sauté until mushrooms are tender and dry, about 8 minutes.

Meanwhile, preheat oven to 425°F. Place bread cut side down on baking sheet. Bake until round sides are lightly toasted, about 5 minutes. Brush cut sides with olive oil and return to oven cut side up until lightly toasted, about 5 minutes. Spread half of marinara sauce over each bread half. Spread half of mushrooms and half of sausage over each. Sprinkle each with half of cheeses. Bake until cheese is golden and bubbly, about 15 minutes. Cut into slices and serve.

# THREE-CHEESE PIZZA

2 SERVINGS; CAN BE DOUBLED

A mixed green salad with herbed vinaigrette makes a good start to this classically simple pizza, with fresh figs and *biscotti* for dessert. (Pictured above.)

| | |
|---|---|
| 1 | 10-ounce tube refrigerated pizza dough |
| 1½ | cups packed shredded mozzarella cheese (about 6 ounces) |
| ½ | cup crumbled Gorgonzola cheese (about 2 ounces) |
| 5 | small plum tomatoes, thinly sliced |
| 1½ | teaspoons dried oregano, crumbled |
| ¼ | cup grated Parmesan cheese (about 1 ounce) |

Position rack in lowest third of oven and preheat to 425°F. Lightly oil 9 x 9-inch pan with 2-inch-high sides. Unroll pizza dough and fit into prepared pan, pressing up at edges to create ½-inch-high border. Sprinkle pizza dough evenly with shredded mozzarella, then with crumbled Gorgonzola cheese. Arrange tomato slices over cheeses. Sprinkle crumbled oregano, then grated Parmesan cheese over.

Bake until cheeses bubble and edges of pizza are brown and crisp, about 30 minutes. Let stand 5 minutes.

Cut slightly cooled pizza into 4 equal squares and serve.

## CHICKEN AND BELL PEPPER PIZZA WITH BARBECUE SAUCE

4 SERVINGS; CAN BE DOUBLED

Go casual here, and serve that tasty standby — sour cream and onion dip with carrots and celery — with the pizza. Purchased ice cream bon bons are a dessert everyone will love.

| | |
|---|---|
| 1½ | cups shredded cooked chicken |
| ¾ | cup spicy or hickory-flavored barbecue sauce |
| 1 | 16-ounce baked cheese pizza crust (such as Boboli) |
| ½ | medium onion, sliced |
| ¼ | green bell pepper, sliced |
| ¼ | red bell pepper, sliced |
| ⅓ | cup thinly sliced drained oil-packed sun-dried tomatoes |
| ¼ | cup pine nuts |
| 2 | teaspoons dried oregano, crumbled |
| 1½ | cups packed shredded mozzarella cheese (about 6 ounces) |

Preheat oven to 450°F. Combine chicken and barbecue sauce in small bowl. Let mixture stand 10 minutes. *(Can be prepared 2 hours ahead. Cover mixture and refrigerate.)*

Place pizza crust on baking sheet. Spread chicken mixture over. Arrange onion, bell peppers, sun-dried tomatoes and pine nuts over. Sprinkle with oregano. Season lightly with salt and pepper. Spread cheese evenly over. Bake pizza until crust is crisp and cheese bubbles, about 17 minutes. Serve immediately.

## TRICOLOR BOBOLI PIZZAS

6 SERVINGS; CAN BE DOUBLED

Begin the meal with a quick soup of canned chicken broth simmered with purchased tortellini and topped with grated Parmesan cheese. End it with pretty parfaits made simply by alternating layers of orange sherbet and cherry pie filling in tall stemmed glasses.

| | |
|---|---|
| ¼ | cup olive oil |
| 2 | large red onions, sliced |
| 2 | large red bell peppers, thinly sliced |
| 2 | 1-pound baked cheese pizza crusts (such as Boboli) |
| ¾ | cup olive paste (olivada)* |
| ½ | pound soft mild goat cheese (such as Montrachet), crumbled |
| ½ | cup chopped fresh oregano |
| ½ | cup toasted pine nuts (about 3 ounces) |

Heat olive oil in heavy large skillet over medium heat. Add sliced red onions and sliced red bell peppers and sauté until beginning to brown, stirring frequently, about 10 minutes. *(Can be prepared 4 hours ahead. Let onion mixture stand at room temperature.)*

Preheat oven to 450°F. Place Boboli on pizza pans or cookie sheets. Spread each Boboli with half of olive paste. Top each with half of onion mixture. Sprinkle with crumbled goat cheese. Bake until cheese softens, about 10 minutes. Remove from oven. Sprinkle with chopped fresh oregano and toasted pine nuts. Cut pizzas into wedges and serve.

*An olive spread available at Italian markets and specialty foods stores. If unavailable, use pureed, pitted, brine-cured black olives.*

# PIZZA WITH CLAMS AND TOMATOES

2 SERVINGS; CAN BE DOUBLED

Set out a big salad of garden lettuces with a light red wine vinegar dressing to go with the pizza; then top off the meal with spumoni ice cream cones.

2　tablespoons olive oil
2　garlic cloves, minced
¼　teaspoon dried crushed red pepper
1　cup packed grated mozzarella cheese (about 4 ounces)
3　tablespoons chopped fresh parsley
2　tablespoons grated Parmesan cheese
1　tablespoon chopped fresh thyme or 1 teaspoon dried, crumbled
1　10-ounce tube refrigerated All Ready Pizza Crust

Nonstick vegetable oil spray
2　large plum tomatoes, thinly sliced
1　6½-ounce can chopped clams, drained

Prepare barbecue (medium heat). Mix oil, garlic and crushed red pepper in small bowl. Let stand 10 minutes. Combine mozzarella, parsley, Parmesan cheese and thyme in medium bowl. Unroll pizza dough on heavy large baking sheet. Stretch dough into 12-inch square. Cut pizza dough into 4 equal squares.

Spray grill rack with vegetable oil spray. Place dough squares on grill rack and grill until tops are dry and set and bottoms are light brown, about 3 minutes. Using spatula, transfer dough, grilled side up, to baking sheet. Brush top of dough with oil mixture. Cover with tomato slices and sprinkle with clams and cheese mixture. Return pizzas to grill, tent with foil and cook until cheeses melt, about 3 minutes. Serve.

❧

# FONTINA, ONION AND GOAT CHEESE PIZZA

4 SERVINGS; CAN BE DOUBLED

Steamed broccoli and cauliflower florets mixed with cherry tomatoes and tossed with a white wine vinaigrette would make a nice accompaniment to this delicious pizza. Hot fudge sundaes would hit the spot for dessert. (Pictured on page 2.)

4　bacon slices
1　red onion, sliced

1　tablespoon cornmeal
10　ounces frozen bread dough, thawed
2½　cups shredded Fontina cheese
1　small tomato, diced
2　ounces goat cheese, crumbled
1　teaspoon minced fresh rosemary or ½ teaspoon dried, crumbled

Preheat oven to 450°F. Sauté bacon in heavy medium skillet until crisp. Transfer bacon to paper towel to drain. Add red onion to skillet and sauté until translucent, about 6 minutes. Crumble bacon.

Sprinkle baking sheet or pizza pan with cornmeal. Roll out dough on lightly floured surface to 12-inch round. Transfer to prepared baking sheet. Top with half of Fontina. Scatter onion, bacon, tomato, goat cheese and rosemary evenly over pizza. Top with remaining Fontina. Season generously with pepper. Bake until crust is golden brown and cheese is golden and bubbly, about 22 minutes.

# Spicy Sausage Calzones

2 SERVINGS; CAN BE DOUBLED

Accompany these pizza turnovers with a salad of fennel and radicchio. Finish with fresh orange and pineapple chunks. (Pictured below.)

8 ounces sweet or hot Italian sausages, casings removed
1 14-ounce jar spicy marinara sauce (about 1½ cups)
⅓ cup part-skim ricotta cheese
1 cup grated mozzarella cheese (about 4 ounces)
1 10-ounce tube refrigerated pizza dough

Preheat oven to 425°F. Lightly grease heavy large baking sheet. Sauté sausage in heavy medium skillet over medium-high heat until cooked through, breaking up with back of spoon, about 8 minutes. Using slotted spoon, transfer sausage to bowl. Add ½ cup marinara sauce and ricotta cheese to sausage and blend. Mix in mozzarella. Season filling to taste with salt and pepper.

Unfold dough on prepared baking sheet. Gently stretch dough to 11- to 12-inch square. Cut dough into 4 even squares. Spoon ¼ of filling into center of each square. Fold dough over filling, forming triangle. Press dough edges together to seal tightly; crimp with tines of fork. Using small sharp knife cut 3 slits in top of each calzone to allow steam to escape. Bake until golden brown, about 15 minutes.

Meanwhile, bring remaining marinara sauce just to simmer in heavy medium saucepan. Transfer calzones to plates; serve with sauce.

# POULTRY

Close to half of any given supermarket meat department is now devoted to poultry — a fact that really makes you realize how much we've changed how we eat in recent years. Consumption of chicken and turkey has soared, based not only on time-saving and convenience factors but also on our awareness of the health benefits associated with poultry's low fat content. Of course, chicken and turkey also happen to taste terrific, with a delicate flavor that appeals to all ages and makes it the perfect medium for adventurous and exotic saucing and seasoning.

Not a month goes by that we don't include a poultry recipe in our *Bon Appétit* column, yet we never seem to come up short when we're coming up with different ways to prepare this versatile food. None of this under-30-minute cooking with chicken would be possible, however if it weren't for that first clever person who (in a veritable act of marketing genius) lopped off parts of the bird, removed skin and bones, wrapped up the pieces and stuck them in the supermarket meat case. Our grandmothers would never have believed that we'd be paying good money for that convenience, but then they likely didn't juggle a full-time job with driving a soccer carpool, doing the laundry and getting dinner on the table every night.

Boneless chicken breasts and thinly sliced chicken and turkey cutlets are perhaps the most versatile poultry parts. When cooked as a simple sauté, seasoned with one of any number of flavors (from mustard to garlic to tarragon), then topped with a quick sauce made by deglazing the pan, the results are simple yet spectacular. From delicate, creamy Spring Chicken (page 54) to

Sautéed Chicken with Buttered Pecans (page 51)

fresh-tasting Turkey Cutlets with Almonds and Snow Peas (page 76), and from tangy, autumnal Turkey Cutlets with Apricot-Cranberry Sauce (page 73) to richly extravagant Sautéed Chicken with Buttered Pecans (page 51), every season and every taste is deliciously represented here.

Turkey, that New World bird, was traditionally used in the American Southwest in combination with fiery chilies and other ingredients indigenous to the region. Here, we offer such streamlined takes on that tradition as piquant Turkey Chili Verde (page 79), along with modern interpretations, including quick and tasty Turkey Tostadas (page 79) and Southwest Turkey and Rice Salad (page 73).

As for game hens, these miniature chickens broil or roast (if cut in half) to crisp, succulent tenderness in just under 30 minutes, and take particularly well to herbal seasoning and/or a brush with a burnishing fruit glaze. The goodness of Roasted Sage-rubbed Cornish Game Hen (page 82) or Broiled Game Hen with Apple-Thyme Glaze (page 80) belies their simplicity.

In the end, if the 30-minute cook had to choose a motto, our vote would likely be: Poultry Gets the Part.

Southwest Turkey and Rice Salad (page 73)

# Sautéed Chicken with Buttered Pecans

2 SERVINGS; CAN BE DOUBLED

Baked sweet potatoes and sautéed zucchini rounds are tasty side dishes. Mixed dried fruit simmered with sugar, water and a cinnamon stick makes a quick and easy dessert compote. (Pictured on page 48.)

2    skinless boneless chicken breast halves
1½   tablespoons butter

¾    teaspoon dried rubbed sage
¼    cup minced shallots
¼    cup broken pecan pieces
⅓    cup dry white wine
⅓    cup canned low-salt chicken broth

Season chicken breast halves with salt and pepper. Melt 1 tablespoon butter in heavy medium skillet over medium-high heat. Add chicken and sauté until just cooked through and beginning to brown, about 3 minutes per side. Transfer chicken to plate.

Add remaining ½ tablespoon butter and sage to skillet. Stir until aromatic, about 15 seconds. Add shallots and pecans and sauté until pecans begin to brown, about 2 minutes. Add wine and broth. Increase heat to high. Boil sauce until reduced to syrup consistency, about 8 minutes. Spoon sauce over chicken.

# Skillet Chicken with Aromatic Vegetables

2 SERVINGS; CAN BE DOUBLED

A mixed green salad with beets, garlic croutons and a simple vinaigrette makes a great intro. Sprinkle some poppy seeds over buttered noodles to serve alongside. Top purchased spice cake with rum-raisin ice cream to finish.

4    skinless boneless chicken thighs (about 10 ounces), each cut into 4 pieces
1    tablespoon olive oil
2    celery stalks, cut into 1-inch pieces
1    cup baby carrots
1    cup diced onion
¾    cup canned low-salt chicken broth
1½   teaspoons dried thyme, crumbled

Season chicken with salt and pepper. Heat oil in heavy medium skillet over medium-high heat. Add chicken to skillet and sauté until light brown, about 3 minutes per side. Add celery, carrots and onion and toss to coat with pan juices. Add broth and thyme. Bring to simmer. Cover and reduce heat to medium-low. Cook until chicken and vegetables are just tender, about 10 minutes. Using slotted spoon, transfer chicken and vegetables to bowl. Increase heat to high and boil liquids until reduced to ¼ cup, about 7 minutes. Return chicken and vegetables to skillet and stir to coat with sauce. Serve hot.

# BROILED LEMON-OREGANO CHICKEN

2 SERVINGS; CAN BE DOUBLED

Broil or sauté an assortment of red, green and yellow bell pepper strips to serve alongside the chicken and complete the main course with orzo (a rice-shaped pasta) tossed with olive oil. Baklava from the bakery and strong coffee finish this Greek-style meal.

| | |
|---|---|
| 1 | large lemon |
| 3 | tablespoons chopped fresh parsley |
| 1½ | teaspoons dried oregano, crumbled |
| ½ | teaspoon pepper |
| 2 | large garlic cloves, chopped |
| ½ | teaspoon salt |
| 2 | chicken breast halves with skin and bones |
| 1 | tablespoon olive oil |
| ½ | cup plain yogurt |

Grate 1½ teaspoons peel from lemon. Cut lemon in half. Cut 2 center slices from 1 half and reserve. Squeeze enough juice from remaining half to make 1 teaspoon. Place lemon peel into small bowl. Add 2 tablespoons parsley, oregano and pepper. Place garlic on cutting board. Sprinkle salt over and chop garlic very finely. Add garlic mixture to seasonings in small bowl. Loosen skin on chicken breasts. Spread generous ½ tablespoon seasoning mixture under skin of of each chicken breast. Rub chicken with oil; season with salt and pepper. Mix yogurt and 1 teaspoon lemon juice into remaining seasoning mixture for sauce. (*Chicken and sauce can be prepared 8 hours ahead. Cover and refrigerate.*)

Preheat broiler or prepare barbecue (medium-high heat). Broil chicken until cooked through, 12 minutes per side. Arrange on plates. Garnish with lemon and parsley. Serve with yogurt sauce.

# EASY CHICKEN AND DUMPLINGS

2 SERVINGS; CAN BE DOUBLED

For a fast first course, try tossing marinated artichoke hearts and their dressing with halved cherry tomatoes and sliced Belgian endive. Top off this comforting meal with cherry pie.

| | |
|---|---|
| 2 | tablespoons (¼ stick) butter |
| 4 | skinless boneless chicken thighs, cut into 2-inch pieces |
| 2 | tablespoons all purpose flour |
| 1 | teaspoon dried thyme, crumbled |
| ⅔ | cup frozen pearl onions |
| 2 | carrots, peeled, thinly sliced |
| 2 | celery stalks, thinly sliced |
| 1½ | cups canned low-salt chicken broth |
| ⅔ | cup buttermilk baking mix |
| ¼ | cup milk |

Melt butter in heavy large Dutch oven over medium heat. Season chicken thighs with salt and pepper. Add chicken to pot and sauté until beginning to color, about 3 minutes. Sprinkle with flour and ½ teaspoon thyme and stir 1 minute. Add pearl onions, carrots, celery and broth and bring to simmer, scraping bottom of pot.

Combine baking mix, milk and ½ teaspoon thyme in small bowl. Stir until soft dough forms. Drop dough by heaping teaspoonfuls onto simmering stew. Cover pot. Reduce heat to medium-low; cook until dumplings are puffed and chicken is cooked 17 minutes. Serve.

# CHICKEN THIGHS WITH MAPLE-MUSTARD GLAZE

2 SERVINGS; CAN BE DOUBLED

Toss fresh spinach with a blue cheese vinaigrette, and mash some cooked winter squash to complement the chicken. Purchased apple turnovers would be a delicious finale. (Pictured below.)

1½  tablespoons vegetable oil
1   large shallot, minced
3   tablespoons pure maple syrup
1½  tablespoons coarse-grained Dijon mustard

4   small skinless chicken thighs

Heat oil in heavy small saucepan over medium heat. Add shallot and sauté until beginning to soften, about 1 minute. Add maple syrup and mustard and simmer until glaze thickens and bubbles, stirring occasionally, 2 minutes. *(Can be prepared 1 day ahead. Cover and chill.)*

Preheat broiler. Season chicken with salt and pepper. Place chicken on small broilerproof pan. Brush with glaze. Broil chicken 5 minutes. Turn chicken over; brush with glaze. Broil until chicken is golden brown and cooked through, about 8 minutes. Transfer chicken to plates. Bring any remaining glaze just to boil and pour over chicken. Serve chicken thighs immediately.

## SPRING CHICKEN

2 SERVINGS; CAN BE DOUBLED

Fettuccine tossed with black pepper is a nice accompaniment. And how about spice cake à la mode for a great finale? (Pictured at right.)

2 large skinless boneless chicken breast halves
½ teaspoon dried tarragon, crumbled

1 tablespoon butter
¼ cup dry white wine
⅓ cup whipping cream
⅔ cup frozen peas and carrots, thawed
¼ cup chopped fresh chives

Place chicken between sheets of plastic wrap. Pound with rolling pin to thickness of ½ inch. Season with salt, pepper and tarragon.

Melt butter in heavy large skillet over high heat. Add chicken breasts and sauté until golden and just cooked through, about 3 minutes per side. Transfer chicken to plate. Add wine to skillet and cook until reduced to glaze, scraping up browned bits, about 2 minutes. Add cream and peas and carrots. Cook until vegetables are tender and sauce has thickened slightly, about 3 minutes. Add chicken and any accumulated juices to pan and cook until chicken is just heated through, about 1 minute. Stir in chives. Divide chicken between plates. Spoon sauce and vegetables over.

## COUNTRY CAPTAIN CHICKEN

4 SERVINGS; CAN BE DOUBLED

After a watercress salad to start, serve rice alongside the chicken, then finish the meal with vanilla ice cream topped with warm caramel sauce.

1 pound skinless boneless chicken thighs (about 4 large)
½ teaspoon salt
½ teaspoon cayenne pepper
2 tablespoons (¼ stick) unsalted butter
1 medium onion, chopped
1 large red bell pepper, seeded, cut into thin strips
2 large garlic cloves, minced
2 teaspoons curry powder
1 14½-ounce can whole tomatoes
¼ cup dried currants
1 teaspoon dried thyme, crumbled

¼ cup toasted slivered almonds

Sprinkle both sides of chicken with salt and cayenne. Melt butter in heavy large skillet over high heat. Add chicken and cook until light brown, about 3 minutes per side. Transfer chicken to plate. Add onion and red bell pepper to same skillet. Reduce heat to medium. Sauté until vegetables begin to soften, about 3 minutes. Add garlic and curry powder and stir 1 minute. Add tomatoes with their juices to skillet, breaking up tomatoes with spoon. Bring to simmer. Return chicken and any juices on plate to skillet. Reduce heat to medium-low. Cover and simmer gently 15 minutes. Uncover, mix in currants and thyme and cook until chicken is tender, 5 minutes. Season with salt and pepper.

Arrange chicken on deep platter. Spoon vegetables and sauce around. Sprinkle with almonds and serve.

## CURRY AND HONEY
## ROAST CHICKEN

2 SERVINGS; CAN BE DOUBLED

To begin, blend chutney with some cream cheese as an instant dip for carrot and celery sticks. Herbed rice and sautéed Swiss chard go well with the entrée. Coconut macaroons would round out this easy meal nicely. (Pictured above.)

2   chicken breast halves with skin and bones
2   chicken thighs or drumsticks
2   garlic cloves, halved
3   tablespoons honey
2   tablespoons dry white wine
1½  teaspoons curry powder
    Chopped fresh chives (optional)

Preheat oven to 450°F. Pat chicken dry. Rub chicken pieces with garlic. Discard garlic. Place chicken on baking sheet. Bring honey, wine and curry powder to boil in heavy small saucepan. Stir until thick, about 2 minutes. Brush chicken pieces with glaze. Roast 10 minutes. Brush chicken pieces with remaining glaze. Continue roasting until cooked through, 10 minutes for breasts and 15 minutes for thighs. Transfer to platter. Sprinkle with chives and serve.

# CHICKEN WITH LEEKS AND MUSHROOMS

4 SERVINGS; CAN BE DOUBLED

Although this chicken recipe is quick to make, the leeks, wild mushrooms, wine and cream turn it into something quite elegant. Complete the menu with saffron rice and steamed fresh broccoli. Serve raspberry sorbet topped with strawberries for dessert.

| | |
|---|---|
| 4 | skinless boneless chicken breast halves (about 1¼ pounds) |
| 2 | tablespoons (¼ stick) butter |
| 1 | tablespoon olive oil |
| 4 | medium leeks, white and pale green parts only, chopped |
| 4 | ounces wild mushrooms or button mushrooms, thickly sliced |
| ½ | cup dry white wine |
| ½ | cup whipping cream |
| 2 | teaspoons chopped fresh tarragon or ½ teaspoon dried, crumbled |
| | Fresh tarragon sprigs (optional) |

Using meat mallet or rolling pin, flatten chicken pieces between sheets of waxed paper to scant ½-inch thickness. Season with salt and pepper. Melt 1 tablespoon butter with 1 tablespoon olive oil in heavy large skillet over medium-high heat. Sauté chicken until light brown, about 2 minutes per side. Transfer to plate.

Add remaining 1 tablespoon butter to same skillet and melt over medium heat. Add leeks and mushrooms and cook until just beginning to color, stirring occasionally, about 5 minutes. Add wine, cream and chopped tarragon and simmer until leek mixture thickens slightly, about 5 minutes. Return chicken and any accumulated juices to skillet and simmer until chicken is just cooked through and leeks are tender, about 5 minutes longer. Adjust seasonings. Arrange chicken on serving platter. Spoon sauce over. Garnish with tarragon sprigs and serve.

# MUSTARD-COATED CHICKEN BREASTS

2 SERVINGS; CAN BE DOUBLED

Team the chicken with buttered egg noodles tossed with green onions, and a sliced-tomato salad. Chocolate mousse makes a lovely dessert.

| | |
|---|---|
| 1½ | tablespoons Dijon mustard |
| 1½ | tablespoons olive oil |
| 1 | garlic clove, minced |
| ¼ | teaspoon (generous) dried tarragon, crumbled |
| 1 | cup fresh whole wheat breadcrumbs |
| 2 | skinless boneless chicken breast halves (about 5 ounces each) |
| | Chopped fresh parsley (optional) |

Preheat oven to 450°F. Lightly oil heavy baking sheet. Whisk together Dijon mustard, olive oil, minced garlic and tarragon in small bowl. Place breadcrumbs in pie pan. Season chicken with salt and pepper. Spread mustard mixture over both sides of chicken. Dip chicken into breadcrumbs, turning to coat completely. Place chicken on prepared baking sheet. Bake until chicken is cooked through and crumb coating is golden brown, about 14 minutes. Transfer chicken to plates. Garnish with parsley, if desired, and serve.

# GRILLED LEMON-PEPPER CHICKEN SALAD

2 SERVINGS; CAN BE DOUBLED

Thickly sliced tomatoes and hot-from-the-oven biscuits go well with this all-American chicken salad. And how about strawberry sundaes to finish?
(Pictured at left.)

5 tablespoons olive oil
3 tablespoons fresh lemon juice
½ teaspoon hot pepper sauce (such as Tabasco)
½ teaspoon dried thyme, crumbled
2 skinless boneless chicken breast halves
4 ⅓- to ½-inch-thick red onion slices

4 cups torn romaine lettuce
½ cup crumbled feta cheese (about 2 ounces)

Whisk olive oil, lemon juice, pepper sauce and thyme to blend in small saucepan. Season dressing to taste with salt and pepper. Arrange chicken and onion slices on plate. Spoon 2 tablespoons dressing over chicken and onions and turn to coat. Let chicken stand 5 minutes. *(Can be prepared up to 4 hours ahead. Cover and refrigerate).*

Prepare barbecue (medium-high heat). Set saucepan with remaining dressing at edge of barbecue to warm. Grill chicken and onion slices until just cooked through, about 4 minutes per side. Transfer chicken and onion to plate. Cut chicken crosswise into thin slices. Separate grilled red onion into rings.

Place lettuce in large bowl. Add chicken and onion. Add warm dressing and toss to coat. Season salad to taste with salt and pepper. Divide salad between 2 plates. Sprinkle half of feta cheese over each.

# THAI-STYLE CHICKEN SALAD

2 SERVINGS; CAN BE DOUBLED

Store-bought roasted chicken is likely to be tender and moist with well-seasoned skin (which you can discard if you're avoiding fat). Serve warm dinner rolls to complement this fragrant salad, and frozen yogurt topped with sliced tropical fruits, coconut and rum for dessert.

3 limes
¼ cup oriental sesame oil
1 tablespoon minced peeled fresh ginger
1 teaspoon curry powder

4 cups mixed salad greens
1 small red bell pepper, thinly sliced
2 cups ½-inch pieces purchased roasted chicken
⅓ cup coarsely chopped honey-roasted peanuts

Grate enough peel from 1 lime to measure ½ teaspoon. Squeeze enough juice from limes to measure 3 tablespoons. Whisk oil, ginger, curry powder and lime juice to blend in small bowl. Season dressing with salt and pepper. Set aside.

Divide greens and red bell pepper between 2 large plates. Heat dressing in heavy medium skillet over medium heat. Add chicken; toss until heated through, about 2 minutes. Spoon chicken and dressing over greens, dividing equally. Sprinkle peanuts over salads and serve.

## CHICKEN BRAISED WITH BACON AND POTATOES

2 SERVINGS; CAN BE DOUBLED

Hearty and appealing, this main course is a quick version of *poularde à la bonne femme*, which in France is usually a whole chicken simmered with potatoes and other vegetables "in the style of a country woman." Add a green salad and end with a trio of sorbets.
(Pictured on page 6.)

2   large red-skinned potatoes (about 12 ounces),
    cut into ¾-inch dice

2   low-salt bacon slices, cut into ½-inch pieces
4   skinless boneless chicken thighs (about 10 ounces)
1   cup frozen pearl onions, thawed, drained
⅓   cup canned low-salt chicken broth
½   teaspoon dried thyme, crumbled
    Chopped fresh parsley

Cook potatoes in medium saucepan of boiling water 4 minutes. Drain thoroughly. Set aside.

Meanwhile, sauté bacon in heavy medium skillet over medium heat until crisp and brown, about 5 minutes. Using slotted spoon, transfer bacon to paper towels and drain. Season chicken generously with pepper. Add to skillet with bacon drippings and cook over medium-high heat until brown, about 2 minutes per side. Reduce heat to low. Add potatoes, onions, broth and thyme. Cover and simmer until chicken is cooked through and potatoes are tender, about 18 minutes. Uncover, sprinkle with bacon and cook until sauce thickens slightly, basting chicken occasionally, about 3 minutes. Garnish with parsley and serve.

## POACHED CHICKEN WITH GREEN SAUCE

2 SERVINGS; CAN BE DOUBLED

Complement this refreshing entrée with crusty sourdough rolls and a salad of sliced tomatoes and red onion on greens. For dessert, how about an assortment of fresh melon wedges?

1   cup parsley leaves
2   tablespoons packed chopped fresh tarragon or
    2 teaspoons dried, crumbled
1   garlic clove
1   teaspoon Dijon mustard
½   cup regular or reduced-calorie mayonnaise

2   skinless boneless chicken breast halves

    Fresh parsley or tarragon sprigs (optional)

Finely chop parsley, tarragon and garlic with mustard in processor. Add mayonnaise and process until almost smooth, occasionally scraping down sides of work bowl. Season with salt and pepper. Transfer sauce to bowl; cover and refrigerate. *(Can be prepared 1 day ahead.)*

Season chicken with salt and pepper. Place in heavy medium skillet. Pour enough cold water over to barely cover. Bring water to simmer over medium heat and poach chicken until just cooked through, about 10 minutes. Transfer chicken to plate and refrigerate until cool, about 10 minutes. Cut chicken crosswise into ¼-inch-thick slices.

Fan chicken slices on plates. Top with sauce. Garnish with parsley or tarragon if desired and serve.

# CHICKEN CUTLETS WITH HERBED CRANBERRY SAUCE

4 SERVINGS; CAN BE DOUBLED

Prepare pecan-studded rice pilaf and brussels sprouts as side dishes, then pass store-bought gingerbread squares topped with whipped cream for a deliciously easy dessert.
(Pictured below.)

| | |
|---|---|
| 4 | boneless chicken breast halves |
| 3 | tablespoons unsalted butter |
| ¼ | cup minced shallots or green onions |
| 1 | large bay leaf, broken into 2 pieces |
| ¼ | cup dry red wine |
| ⅔ | cup canned whole-berry cranberry sauce |
| ½ | cup canned low-salt chicken broth |
| 1 | tablespoon balsamic vinegar or red wine vinegar |
| | Bay leaves (optional) |

Season chicken on both sides with salt and pepper. Melt 2 tablespoons butter in heavy large skillet over medium-high heat. Add chicken and cook until golden and just cooked through, about 4 minutes per side. Transfer chicken to plate.

Melt remaining 1 tablespoon butter in same skillet. Add shallots and 1 bay leaf and sauté 1 minute. Add wine and bring to boil, scraping up browned bits. Boil until mixture reduces to thick glaze, about 4 minutes. Add cranberry sauce, broth and vinegar and cook until sauce thickens slightly, about 3 minutes. Return chicken and any accumulated juices to skillet. Simmer until chicken is heated through, about 1 minute. Season sauce with salt and pepper. Remove bay leaf pieces. Transfer chicken to platter. Spoon sauce over. Garnish with additional bay leaves.

# QUICK
# COQ AU VIN

2 SERVINGS; CAN BE DOUBLED

Serve buttered egg noodles and broccoli spears with this streamlined classic, and a purchased apple tart afterward. (Pictured at right.)

| 2 | bacon slices |
|---|---|
| 2 | skinless boneless chicken breast halves |
| | All purpose flour |
| ¾ | cup frozen pearl onions |
| ⅔ | cup dry red wine |
| ⅓ | cup canned low-salt chicken broth |
| ¾ | teaspoon dried thyme, crumbled |

Cook bacon in heavy medium skillet over medium heat until crisp and brown. Transfer bacon to paper towel and drain. Crumble.

Season chicken with salt and pepper. Coat with flour; shake off excess. Add chicken to same skillet and sauté over medium heat until chicken is brown and just cooked through, about 4 minutes per side. Using tongs, transfer chicken to plate.

Pour off all but 1 tablespoon fat from skillet. Add onions, wine, broth and thyme to skillet. Bring to boil, scraping up browned bits. Reduce heat to medium-low and simmer until onions are tender and sauce thickens slightly, about 12 minutes; season with salt and pepper. Return chicken and any accumulated juices to skillet. Simmer chicken until just heated through, about 2 minutes. Transfer chicken to plates. Spoon sauce over. Garnish with bacon.

❧

# CHICKEN SAUTÉ
# WITH MUSHROOMS
# AND WHITE WINE

2 SERVINGS; CAN BE DOUBLED

Other wild mushrooms, like chanterelles, oyster mushrooms or even the standard button variety, can be substituted successfully for the shiitake in this recipe. Rice pilaf and green beans are fine accompaniments. Chocolate cake would round out the meal.

| 2 | tablespoons olive oil |
|---|---|
| 2 | large skinless boneless chicken breast halves (about 10 ounces) |
| 4 | ounces fresh shiitake mushrooms, stems trimmed, thinly sliced |
| ¼ | cup chopped shallots |
| ½ | cup canned low-salt chicken broth |
| ¼ | cup dry white wine |
| ½ | teaspoon dried tarragon, crumbled |

Heat 1 tablespoon oil in heavy medium skillet over medium-high heat. Season chicken with salt and pepper. Add chicken to pan and sauté until golden brown and just cooked through, about 5 minutes per side. Transfer chicken to plate.

Heat remaining 1 tablespoon oil in same skillet. Add mushrooms and shallots; sauté until mushrooms are light brown and wilted, 5 minutes. Using slotted spoon, transfer mushroom mixture to plate with chicken. Add broth, wine and tarragon to skillet; simmer until reduced to sauce consistency, 5 minutes. Return chicken, mushrooms and any collected juices to pan. Simmer until just heated through, about 2 minutes. Season with salt and pepper.

# MEDITERRANEAN CHICKEN SALAD SANDWICH

2 SERVINGS; CAN BE DOUBLED

Potato chips and *cornichon* pickles are good with this one. Brandy-poached peaches would top off an easy meal. (Pictured above.)

1½ cups (about 6 ounces) diced cooked chicken
½ cup diced black or green olives (preferably brine-cured)
½ cup chopped red bell pepper
⅓ cup chopped green onion
¼ cup regular or reduced-calorie mayonnaise
1 tablespoon red wine vinegar
1 garlic clove, minced
½ teaspoon dried oregano, crumbled

½ 16-ounce long French bread loaf

Combine chicken, olives, red pepper and green onions in medium bowl. Whisk mayonnaise, vinegar, garlic and oregano to blend in small bowl. Add dressing to salad and toss to coat evenly. Season chicken salad to taste with salt and pepper.

Cut bread in half lengthwise. Remove some bread from top and bottom halves, forming shallow cavity. Spoon salad into cavity of bottom half, spreading evenly. Cover with bread top and press to compact slightly. Cut loaf into 2-inch sections.

# CHICKEN AND ARUGULA SANDWICHES

2 SERVINGS; CAN BE DOUBLED

This is just as good made with turkey breast cutlets. Offer french-fried potatoes or onion rings and lemonade alongside, then finish with fresh cherries.

| | |
|---|---|
| 2 | skinless boneless chicken breast halves |
| 1½ | tablespoons olive oil |
| 1 | green onion, thinly sliced |
| 3 | tablespoons dry white wine |
| ¼ | cup reduced-calorie or regular mayonnaise |
| 4 | thin French bread slices (about 5 inches diameter), toasted |
| 1 | bunch arugula or watercress, stems trimmed |
| 6 | thin tomato slices |

Arrange chicken between sheets of waxed paper. Using rolling pin, gently pound to ⅓-inch thickness. Season with salt and pepper.

Heat olive oil in heavy medium skillet over medium-high heat. Add chicken breast halves and sauté until golden and cooked through, about 3 minutes per side. Transfer chicken to plate. Reduce heat to medium-low. Add half of green onion to skillet and cook 1 minute. Add white wine and cook until reduced to glaze, stirring up browned bits, about 1 minute. Scrape glaze into small bowl. Add mayonnaise and remaining green onion to glaze and whisk until smooth.

Spread mayonnaise mixture on 2 bread slices, dividing evenly. Arrange arugula over. Place one chicken fillet on each sandwich. Place tomatoes over chicken. Top each sandwich with second bread slice.

# MULLIGATAWNY SOUP

2 SERVINGS; CAN BE DOUBLED

This soup was introduced to Britain in the eighteenth century by colonialists returning from India. As accompaniments, serve a watercress salad, along with pita triangles and an easy dip of yogurt mixed with chopped cucumbers and a little ground cumin. End with a coconut layer cake.

| | |
|---|---|
| 2 | tablespoons (¼ stick) butter |
| ½ | cup chopped onion |
| 1 | cup chopped red bell pepper |
| 1 | cup chopped unpeeled tart green apple |
| 1 | tablespoon curry powder |
| 2 | 14½-ounce cans low-salt chicken broth |
| ⅓ | cup long-grain white rice |
| 8 | ounces boneless chicken, cut into ½-inch cubes |

Melt butter in heavy medium saucepan over medium heat. Add onion and sauté until just tender, about 5 minutes. Add bell pepper, apple and curry powder and sauté 2 minutes. Add broth and rice and bring to simmer. Reduce heat to low, partially cover pan and cook soup until rice is almost tender, about 15 minutes. Add chicken. Cook uncovered until rice and chicken are tender, stirring occasionally, about 5 minutes. Serve soup immediately.

## STIR-FRIED CHICKEN WITH ASPARAGUS

2 SERVINGS; CAN BE DOUBLED

This dish can be accompanied by brown rice, white rice or buckwheat noodles. Toss sliced radishes with seasoned rice vinegar for a light salad to start, and offer bowls of orange sherbet and gingersnap cookies for dessert. (Pictured at left.)

| | |
|---|---|
| 8 | to 10 ounces skinless boneless chicken breasts, sliced crosswise into generous ¼-inch-wide strips |
| 1½ | teaspoons ground coriander |
| 2 | tablespoons vegetable oil |
| 20 | slender asparagus spears, trimmed, cut into 1½-inch pieces |
| ½ | cup canned low-salt chicken broth |
| 2 | teaspoons fresh lemon juice |
| ⅓ | cup chopped green onions |
| 1 | teaspoon grated lemon peel |

Toss chicken and coriander together in medium bowl. Season with pepper. *(Can be made 3 hours ahead. Cover and chill.)*

Heat oil in heavy medium skillet over high heat. Add chicken breast and stir-fry until just cooked through, about 2 minutes. Using slotted spoon, transfer chicken to plate. Add asparagus and chicken broth to skillet and cook until asparagus is just tender and broth is reduced by ⅔, about 4 minutes. Return chicken to skillet. Mix in lemon juice. Season with salt and pepper. Add green onions and lemon peel; toss to blend. Serve immediately.

## CHINESE CHICKEN WITH SUMMER VEGETABLES

2 SERVINGS; CAN BE DOUBLED

Peak-season vegetables team up with sliced chicken breasts in this Asian-style dish. Accompany it with steamed rice or crisp Chinese noodles. Serve tangerines and fortune cookies afterward.

| | |
|---|---|
| 3 | tablespoons peanut oil |
| 1 | tablespoon oriental sesame oil |
| 2 | skinless boneless chicken breast halves (about 8 ounces), cut crosswise into thin strips |
| ½ | large red bell pepper, cut into thin 2-inch-long strips |
| 2 | medium-size yellow crookneck squash, halved lengthwise, cut crosswise into thin slices |
| 4 | large green onions, thinly sliced |
| 1 | tablespoon minced peeled fresh ginger |
| 1½ | teaspoons minced garlic |
| 3 | tablespoons canned low-salt chicken broth |
| 1 | tablespoon soy sauce |

Heat peanut and sesame oils in heavy large skillet over high heat. Season chicken with salt and pepper. Add chicken to skillet and stir-fry until just cooked through and beginning to brown, about 2 minutes. Using slotted spoon, transfer chicken to plate. Add red pepper and squash to skillet and stir-fry 2 minutes. Add green onions, ginger and garlic and stir 1 minute. Return chicken to skillet. Add broth and soy sauce and stir 30 seconds. Season to taste with salt and pepper. Transfer to platter and serve immediately.

# CHICKEN IN RED PEPPER SAUCE

4 SERVINGS; CAN BE DOUBLED

For a first course, enrich some canned mushroom soup with fresh sautéed mushrooms. Wide noodles tossed with butter and fresh thyme would be nice alongside the chicken, and for dessert, pick up an apple strudel at the bakery.

| | |
|---|---|
| 1 | tablespoon unsalted butter |
| 1 | tablespoon olive oil |
| 4 | skinless boneless chicken breast halves |
| 1 | onion, chopped |
| 2 | large garlic cloves, chopped |
| 1 | 7½-ounce jar roasted red peppers, drained, chopped |
| 1 | teaspoon paprika |
| ¼ | teaspoon dried crushed red pepper |
| ¾ | cup canned chicken broth |
| ½ | cup whipping cream |
| ½ | teaspoon red wine vinegar |

Melt butter with oil in heavy large skillet over medium-high heat. Season chicken with salt and pepper. Add to skillet and sauté until brown, about 4 minutes per side. Transfer chicken to plate. Add onion and garlic to same skillet and sauté until tender, about 8 minutes. Mix in roasted peppers, paprika and crushed red pepper. Add broth and cream and boil until sauce thickens slightly, stirring frequently, about 5 minutes. Transfer sauce to blender and puree. Return sauce to skillet. Add vinegar and season to taste with salt and pepper. Return chicken and any accumulated juices to sauce. Simmer over medium heat until cooked through, 2 minutes. Transfer chicken to plates. Spoon sauce over.

# NEW MEXICO CHICKEN STEW

2 SERVINGS; CAN BE DOUBLED

Corn bread and steamed Swiss chard sprinkled with pine nuts would go well with the stew; follow that with sugar cookies and sherbet or sorbet.

| | |
|---|---|
| 1 | tablespoon olive oil |
| 2 | boneless chicken breast halves |
| 1 | teaspoon ground cumin |
| 2 | large garlic cloves, chopped |
| 1 | 14½-ounce can chili-style chunky tomatoes |
| ¾ | cup drained canned golden hominy |
| 2 | tablespoons canned diced green chilies |
| 4 | tablespoons chopped fresh cilantro |

Heat oil in heavy medium skillet over medium-high heat. Season chicken with cumin, salt and pepper. Add chicken to skillet; sauté until brown, about 3 minutes per side. Reduce heat to medium-low. Add garlic; sauté 30 seconds. Add tomatoes, hominy, green chilies and 2 tablespoons cilantro. Simmer uncovered until juices thicken slightly and chicken is just cooked through, turning chicken once, about 7 minutes. Transfer chicken to platter; spoon sauce over. Garnish with 2 tablespoons cilantro and serve.

# CHICKEN TORTELLINI SOUP WITH SPINACH

2 SERVINGS; CAN BE DOUBLED

A mini antipasto of caponata, roasted peppers, olives and a loaf of seeded Italian bread makes a nice partner for the soup. Serve orange slices drizzled with amaretto for an Italian-style finish. (Pictured below.)

| | |
|---|---|
| 2 | tablespoons olive oil |
| 4 | ounces mushrooms, thinly sliced |
| 2 | large garlic cloves, chopped |
| 3 | 14½-ounce cans low-salt chicken broth |
| 1 | 9-ounce package fresh chicken and vegetable tortellini |
| 3 | cups thinly sliced ready-to-use spinach leaves (about 5 ounces) |
| 2 | tablespoons grated Parmesan cheese |

Additional grated Parmesan cheese

Heat oil in heavy large saucepan over medium heat. Add mushrooms and garlic; sauté until mushrooms are tender, about 5 minutes. Add broth and bring to boil. Add tortellini, cover pan partially and boil until tortellini are tender but still firm to bite, about 5 minutes. Add spinach and simmer until wilted, about 2 minutes. Mix in 2 tablespoons cheese. Season soup with salt and pepper.

Ladle soup into bowls. Serve soup, passing additional grated Parmesan cheese separately.

# AMERICAN COUNTRY CHICKEN FRICASSEE

2 SERVINGS; CAN BE DOUBLED

Begin with a chicory salad in cider vinaigrette. Pass warm buttermilk biscuits with the main course, and stay old-fashioned with an apple pie and wedges of cheddar cheese for dessert. (Pictured at right.)

| | |
|---|---|
| 2 | boneless chicken breast halves |
| 2 | tablespoons all purpose flour |
| 2 | tablespoons vegetable oil |
| ½ | onion, thinly sliced |
| 1 | cup canned stewed tomatoes with juices |
| ½ | cup frozen baby lima beans, thawed |
| ⅓ | cup canned chicken broth |
| 1 | teaspoon Worcestershire sauce |
| ½ | teaspoon dried thyme, crumbled |
| ¼ | teaspoon hot pepper sauce (such as Tabasco) |
| ½ | cup frozen corn kernels, thawed |

Season chicken with salt and pepper. Dredge in flour. Shake off excess. Heat 1 tablespoon oil in heavy medium skillet over medium-high heat. Add chicken and sauté until golden, about 3 minutes per side. Transfer to plate and then set aside.

Add remaining 1 tablespoon oil and onion to skillet. Sauté until onion begins to soften, about 3 minutes. Return chicken to skillet. Add tomatoes, lima beans, broth, Worcestershire, thyme and pepper sauce. Bring to boil. Reduce heat to low, cover and simmer until chicken is cooked through and lima beans are tender, about 8 minutes. Add corn; simmer uncovered until corn is tender, about 2 minutes. Transfer chicken to platter. Simmer sauce until thickened slightly, about 5 minutes. Season with salt and pepper. Spoon sauce over chicken and serve.

# CHICKEN WITH RICE AND SPANISH OLIVES

2 SERVINGS; CAN BE DOUBLED

Offer a salad of sliced tomatoes with this hearty main course, then sliced oranges to complete an easy meal. If you double the recipe, use a large skillet.

| | |
|---|---|
| 2 | tablespoons olive oil |
| 2 | large boneless chicken thighs, each cut into 4 pieces |
| 1 | medium onion, coarsely chopped |
| ½ | cup diced smoked ham |
| 2 | large garlic cloves, minced |
| ½ | cup medium- or short-grain white rice |
| 1 | cup water |
| ½ | cup sliced small green pimiento-stuffed olives |

Heat oil in heavy medium skillet over high heat. Season chicken with pepper. Sauté until golden brown, about 5 minutes. Using tongs, transfer chicken to plate. Reduce heat to medium. Add onion and ham to skillet and sauté until onion is soft, about 4 minutes. Add garlic and rice and stir 1 minute. Add water, chicken and any accumulated juices to skillet. Bring to simmer. Cover, reduce heat to low and cook until rice is tender and chicken is cooked through, about 20 minutes. Mix in olives. Season with salt and pepper. Serve immediately.

# SOUTHWEST TURKEY AND RICE SALAD

4 SERVINGS; CAN BE DOUBLED

Instead of white rice, you can use brown rice, orzo (rice-shaped pasta) or any other small pasta. Serve hot flour tortillas with butter alongside the colorful salad, then finish with sliced fruit and a bakery angel food cake. (Pictured at left.)

| | |
|---|---|
| 1½ | cups water |
| 1 | cup long-grain white rice |
| 2 | cups diced cooked turkey or chicken |
| ¾ | pound ripe plum tomatoes, seeded, diced |
| 1 | cup thinly sliced green bell pepper |
| 1 | cup corn kernels, cooked fresh or frozen, thawed |
| ⅓ | cup chopped red onion |
| | |
| ½ | cup olive oil |
| 6 | tablespoons chopped fresh cilantro |
| 3 | tablespoons white wine vinegar |
| 1 | tablespoon Dijon mustard |
| 1 | large jalapeño chili, seeded if desired, minced |
| 1¼ | teaspoons ground cumin |
| ¾ | teaspoon salt |
| ¾ | teaspoon pepper |
| | Red leaf lettuce |
| 1 | ripe avocado, peeled, sliced |

Bring 1½ cups water to boil in heavy medium saucepan. Mix in long-grain white rice. Cover and cook over low heat until rice is just tender, about 18 minutes. Transfer rice to large bowl. Add turkey, tomatoes, green bell pepper, corn and onion; toss.

Whisk together olive oil, cilantro, vinegar, mustard, chili, cumin, salt and pepper. Pour dressing over salad and mix gently. *(Can be prepared 3 hours ahead. Cover and refrigerate.)* Arrange lettuce on platter. Mound salad in center. Garnish with avocado.

# TURKEY CUTLETS WITH APRICOT-CRANBERRY SAUCE

2 SERVINGS; CAN BE DOUBLED

Sautéed zucchini chunks and rice pilaf are great accompaniments. A purchased almond tart finishes this dinner nicely.

| | |
|---|---|
| 2 | tablespoons olive oil |
| 1½ | teaspoons dried rubbed sage |
| 8 | to 10 ounces turkey breast cutlets |
| 3 | tablespoons chopped shallots |
| 3 | tablespoons dried cranberries (about 1 ounce) |
| ¼ | cup sliced dried apricots (about 1½ ounces) |
| ½ | cup canned low-salt chicken broth |
| ⅓ | cup dry white wine |

Stir oil and sage in heavy medium skillet over low heat until fragrant, about 2 minutes. Increase heat to high. Season turkey cutlets with salt and pepper. Sauté until just cooked through, about 1 minute per side. Transfer turkey to plate. Add shallots to same skillet and sauté 30 seconds. Add cranberries, apricots, broth and wine and simmer until fruit is tender and sauce reduces slightly, about 4 minutes. Return turkey to skillet and cook until just warmed through, about 30 seconds.

Transfer turkey to platter. Spoon sauce over turkey and serve.

# Herbed Turkey Burgers

2 SERVINGS; CAN BE DOUBLED

Add color to the plate by teaming the burgers with fresh corn on the cob and steamed green beans. A slice of peach pie would be nice for dessert. (Pictured below.)

8   ounces ground turkey
½   cup fresh whole wheat breadcrumbs
2   green onions, chopped
1½  tablespoons chopped fresh dill or 1½ teaspoons dried dillweed
1½  teaspoons Dijon mustard
1   egg white, beaten to blend
¼   teaspoon salt
¼   teaspoon ground pepper

    Nonstick vegetable oil spray
2   poppy seed kaiser rolls or buns, split
    Dijon mustard
2   lettuce leaves
2   large tomato slices

Prepare barbecue (medium-high heat). Combine turkey, breadcrumbs, green onions, dill, 1½ teaspoons mustard, egg white, salt and pepper in large bowl. Using hands, mix thoroughly. Shape turkey mixture into two 4-inch-diameter patties, each about ½ inch thick.

Spray grill rack generously with vegetable oil spray. Grill turkey burgers until white in center but still juicy, about 6 minutes per side. Place kaiser rolls, cut side down, at edge of grill and toast lightly, about 2 minutes. Transfer kaiser rolls to plates. Spread bottom half of each roll with Dijon mustard. Top with lettuce leaf, burger, tomato slice and top of roll and serve immediately.

## CONTEMPORARY CLUB SANDWICH

2 SERVINGS; CAN BE DOUBLED

We like potato chips and pickles (or pickled vegetables) with the sandwich. For a cool finish, try vanilla frozen yogurt topped with sliced peaches.

⅓   cup regular or reduced-calorie mayonnaise
2   tablespoons minced chives or green onion tops
½   teaspoon dried tarragon

5   bacon slices, cut in half

6   thin slices whole wheat bread, lightly toasted
4   thin slices tomato
¼   pound thinly sliced roast turkey
½   bunch watercress, stems trimmed

Combine mayonnaise, chives and tarragon in small bowl. *(Can be prepared 1 day ahead. Cover and refrigerate.)*

Cook bacon in heavy large skillet over medium heat until brown and crisp. Transfer to paper towels and drain.

Spread 1 side of each bread slice with herb mayonnaise. Arrange bacon and tomato atop mayonnaise on 2 bread slices. Top each with second bread slice. Arrange turkey and watercress over. Top each sandwich with third bread slice, mayonnaise side down. Cut each sandwich in half diagonally. Secure with toothpicks.

## TURKEY AND MIXED VEGETABLE STIR-FRY

2 SERVINGS; CAN BE DOUBLED

Here's a clever preparation for leftover turkey. For dessert, pass a plate of gingersnaps to go with mandarin orange segments and pineapple chunks.

½   cup canned low-salt chicken broth
2   tablespoons reduced-sodium soy sauce
¾   teaspoon cornstarch

1   tablespoon oriental sesame oil
3   cups broccoli florets (about 5 ounces)
½   large red bell pepper, seeded, sliced
2   cups diced cooked turkey (preferably dark meat)
1   tablespoon chopped peeled fresh ginger
1   large garlic clove, minced

Combine first 3 ingredients in small bowl. Stir until cornstarch dissolves and mixture is smooth. Set aside.

Heat oil in wok or large nonstick skillet over medium-high heat. Add broccoli and bell pepper; stir-fry until broccoli turns bright green and browns in spots, about 3 minutes. Add turkey, ginger and garlic; stir-fry until ginger and garlic are aromatic, about 1 minute. Stir soy sauce mixture and add to pan. Toss until sauce boils and thickens, about 2 minutes. Season with pepper and serve.

# Turkey Cutlets with Almonds and Snow Peas

4 SERVINGS; CAN BE DOUBLED

Here we spotlight turkey cutlets with spring-green snow peas and herbs. Round out the main course with dinner rolls and saffron rice. Indulge yourself afterward with rich chocolate ice cream sprinkled with raspberries. (Pictured at right.)

| | |
|---|---|
| 1 | pound turkey breast cutlets (about ¼ to ⅓ inch thick) |
| 4 | tablespoons (½ stick) butter |
| ⅓ | cup sliced almonds (about 1 ounce) |
| 3 | garlic cloves, minced |
| 12 | ounces snow peas, trimmed, halved diagonally |
| 1 | tablespoon minced fresh tarragon or ½ teaspoon dried, crumbled |
| ½ | cup dry white wine |

Pat turkey dry with paper towels. Season with salt and pepper. Melt 2 tablespoons butter in heavy large skillet over high heat. Add turkey to skillet and fry until light golden and just cooked through, about 1 minute per side. Transfer turkey to platter. Tent with foil.

Reduce heat to medium. Melt 1 tablespoon more butter in same skillet. Add almonds and sauté until golden, stirring constantly, about 30 seconds. Using slotted spoon, transfer almonds to small dish. Melt remaining 1 tablespoon butter in same skillet. Add garlic and stir to coat with butter. Add snow peas and tarragon and sauté until snow peas are just tender, about 2 minutes. Arrange snow pea mixture over turkey. Pour wine into skillet and boil until liquid is slightly reduced, scraping up any browned bits, about 3 minutes. Season sauce to taste with salt and pepper. Spoon sauce over turkey and snow peas. Sprinkle almonds over and serve immediately.

# Turkey with Country Pan Gravy

2 SERVINGS; CAN BE DOUBLED

This entrée would be good with green peas, salad and buttermilk biscuits; offer applesauce and cookies to finish.

| | |
|---|---|
| 8 | ounces turkey breast cutlets or slices |
| 1 | teaspoon poultry seasoning |
| 2 | tablespoons (¼ stick) unsalted butter |
| 2 | green onions, thinly sliced |
| 4 | teaspoons all purpose flour |
| ¾ | cup canned low-salt chicken broth |

Season cutlets with ½ teaspoon poultry seasoning, salt and pepper. Melt 1 tablespoon butter in heavy medium skillet over medium-high heat. Add turkey and sauté until just cooked through, about 2 minutes per side. Transfer turkey to plates. Add remaining 1 tablespoon butter and green onions to same skillet and sauté until onions are soft, about 1 minute. Add flour and remaining ½ teaspoon poultry seasoning and stir 1 minute. Gradually whisk in broth. Cook until gravy boils and thickens, whisking constantly, about 2 minutes. Season with salt and pepper. Pour gravy over turkey.

# TURKEY TOSTADAS

4 SERVINGS; CAN BE DOUBLED

Top the tostadas with a bit of sour cream, and set out sliced avocados, bottled salsa, chopped olives and shredded lettuce. Chocolate pudding makes an easy dessert.
(Pictured at left.)

| | |
|---|---|
| 8 | 6- to 7-inch flour tortillas |
| 1 | 16-ounce can refried beans |
| 2½ | teaspoons chili powder |
| 1 | teaspoon ground cumin |
| 3½ | cups diced cooked turkey (about 1 pound) |
| 1 | cup chopped green onions (about 3 large) |
| 1 | cup chopped plum tomatoes |
| 2 | cups packed shredded Monterey Jack cheese (about 8 ounces) |
| 2 | fresh jalapeño chilies, thinly sliced |

Preheat oven to 425°F. Arrange tortillas on 2 large baking sheets. Bake until crisp and just beginning to color at edges, 5 minutes.

Meanwhile, heat refried beans, 1 teaspoon chili powder and ½ teaspoon cumin in heavy small saucepan over medium heat, stirring constantly. Combine turkey, green onions, tomatoes and remaining ½ teaspoon cumin in medium bowl. Season with salt and pepper.

Spread about ¼ cup warm bean mixture over each tortilla to within 1 inch of edge. Spoon turkey mixture over. Sprinkle with cheese, jalapeño slices and remaining 1½ teaspoons chili powder. Bake tostadas until cheese melts and filling is heated through, about 7 minutes. Transfer 2 tostadas to each plate.

❧

# TURKEY CHILI VERDE

2 SERVINGS; CAN BE DOUBLED

Serve this lively chili with warm tortillas and a colorful plate of sliced avocado, tomato and red onion drizzled with lemon juice. For dessert, tropical fruits, such as mangoes and bananas, drizzled with rum and lime would be refreshing.

| | |
|---|---|
| 1 | tablespoon vegetable oil |
| 8 | ounces turkey breast strips, cut into ½-inch-long pieces |
| 1 | tablespoon cornmeal |
| ¾ | teaspoon ground cumin |
| 1 | cup chopped green onions |
| 1 | cup (or more) canned low-salt chicken broth |
| ¼ | cup canned diced green chilies |
| ¼ | cup chopped fresh cilantro |
| | Cooked white rice |

Heat oil in heavy medium saucepan over high heat. Add turkey and sauté until just golden, about 2 minutes. Reduce heat to medium. Sprinkle cornmeal and cumin over turkey and stir 1 minute. Add green onions and stir just until fragrant, about 30 seconds. Add 1 cup broth and chilies and simmer until thickened, about 5 minutes. *(Can be prepared 1 day ahead. Cover and refrigerate. Rewarm over low heat, thinning with additional broth, if desired.)* Mix in chopped cilantro and simmer 30 seconds. Serve turkey chili over rice.

# BROILED GAME HEN WITH APPLE-THYME GLAZE

2 SERVINGS; CAN BE DOUBLED

Accompany with baked winter squash and buttered, steamed cauliflower. For a great finale: crumb cake topped with scoops of vanilla ice cream.

3 teaspoons olive oil
1 tablespoon minced shallot
2 tablespoons apple jelly
1 teaspoon chopped fresh thyme or ½ teaspoon dried, crumbled
2 teaspoons cider vinegar

1 large Cornish game hen (about 1½ pounds), cut in half, backbone discarded

Apple slices (optional)
Fresh thyme sprigs (optional)

Preheat broiler. Heat 2 teaspoons oil in heavy small saucepan over low heat. Add shallot and sauté until translucent, about 2 minutes. Add apple jelly and chopped thyme and stir until jelly melts. Mix in cider vinegar. Set apple glaze aside.

Rub hen halves with remaining 1 teaspoon oil. Season with salt and pepper. Place hen halves skin side down in broiler pan. Broil about 5 inches from heat source until brown and crisp, 10 minutes. Brush glaze over. Turn hen halves over. Broil skin side up until just cooked through and juices from thigh run clear when pierced, 5 minutes. Brush skin with glaze and broil just until glaze begins to color, about 1 minute.

Arrange hen halves on plates. Garnish with apple slices and thyme sprigs, if desired. Serve immediately.

❧

# HERB-SCENTED GAME HEN WITH WHITE WINE

2 SERVINGS; CAN BE DOUBLED

The flavor of Johannisberg Riesling combines with fresh thyme in both the glaze and the pan juices for the game hen. Serve this dish with rice and a watercress and roasted pepper salad. Raspberries and thin sugar cookies would be a good dessert.

1 1¾-pound game hen, halved, backbone discarded

1 tablespoon butter
1 shallot, minced
¾ cup Johannisberg Riesling or other semisweet white wine
4 teaspoons chopped fresh thyme or 1½ teaspoons dried, crumbled

¼ cup canned low-salt chicken broth

Preheat oven to 450°F. Sprinkle hen halves with salt and pepper. Place skin side up in shallow roasting pan and roast 10 minutes.

Meanwhile, melt butter in heavy small saucepan over medium-high heat. Add shallot and sauté 30 seconds. Add ½ cup wine and thyme and boil until glaze is reduced to 6 tablespoons, about 3 minutes.

Spoon glaze over hen halves. Add remaining ¼ cup wine and chicken broth to roasting pan. Continue roasting until hen halves are brown and juices run clear when thickest part of thigh is pierced, basting occasionally with pan juices, 18 minutes. Serve with pan juices.

# Orange Game Hen with Cumberland Sauce

2 SERVINGS; CAN BE DOUBLED

The streamlined English Cumberland sauce also serves as a glaze. Rice pilaf and brussels sprouts would be nice alongside, and a purchased plum pudding with whipped cream would make the perfect festive dessert.
(Pictured below.)

| | |
|---|---|
| I | large orange |
| I | 1½- to 1¾-pound Cornish game hen, cut into quarters |
| ½ | cup ruby Port |
| 2 | tablespoons red currant jelly |
| 2½ | teaspoons Dijon mustard |
| 2 | teaspoons red wine vinegar |

Preheat oven to 450°F. Cut two ⅛-inch-thick slices from orange; cut slices in half. Grate enough peel from remaining orange to measure ½ teaspoon and squeeze enough juice to measure 2 tablespoons; set aside. Run fingers under skin of hen quarters to loosen and insert 1 half-slice of orange under skin of each. Season with salt and pepper. Arrange on shallow baking pan. Roast 15 minutes.

Meanwhile, combine Port, jelly and orange juice in heavy small saucepan. Bring to boil over medium-high heat, stirring until jelly melts. Reduce heat; simmer until reduced to syrup consistency, about 8 minutes. Remove from heat. Mix in mustard, vinegar and orange peel.

Brush hen pieces with sauce. Roast until juices run clear when thighs are pierced, 10 minutes. Transfer hen pieces to plates. Boil sauce until slightly thickened, about 2 minutes. Spoon sauce over hens.

# ROASTED SAGE-RUBBED CORNISH GAME HEN

2 SERVINGS; CAN BE DOUBLED

Sautéed zucchini strips and couscous pilaf with red bell pepper are good go-withs, and lemon sorbet with walnut cookies makes a lovely dessert.

⅓ cup currant jelly
¼ cup sweet dessert wine (such as Johannisberg Riesling)
1½ teaspoons dried rubbed sage
½ teaspoon dried thyme, crumbled

1 1½-pound Cornish game hen, split in half, backbone discarded
2 teaspoons olive oil

Preheat oven to 450°F. Stir jelly, wine, ½ teaspoon dried sage and thyme in heavy small saucepan over medium heat until jelly dissolves. Simmer until glaze is reduced to scant ½ cup, about 3 minutes.

Season Cornish game hen halves with remaining 1 teaspoon dried sage, salt and pepper. Place skin side up on rack on baking sheet. Brush each half with 1 teaspoon olive oil. Bake until cooked through, basting frequently with 6 tablespoons glaze, about 25 minutes. Spoon remaining 2 tablespoons glaze over and serve.

# SAUTÉED DUCK WITH SOUR CHERRY SAUCE

2 SERVINGS; CAN BE DOUBLED

Serve this elegant yet easy-to-prepare dish with wild rice and steamed green beans. Wedges of pear, sprinkled with walnuts and chunks of Gorgonzola cheese, would make a fine ending.

2 boneless duck breast halves, trimmed of excess fat
¼ teaspoon allspice
¾ cup canned low-salt chicken broth
⅓ cup dried tart pitted cherries
¼ cup brandy
1 teaspoon minced fresh thyme or ¼ teaspoon dried, crumbled

1 tablespoon butter
1 large shallot, minced
¼ cup whipping cream

Rub duck breasts with allspice. Season with salt and pepper. Combine chicken broth, dried cherries, brandy and thyme in heavy small saucepan. Cover and simmer over low heat until cherries are plump and tender, approximately 8 minutes.

Melt butter in heavy medium skillet over medium-high heat. Add duck breasts to skillet skin side down and cook until brown, about 10 minutes. Turn and cook about 4 minutes longer for medium-rare. Transfer duck breasts to plate. Pour off all but 1 tablespoon fat from skillet. Add shallot to skillet and stir 30 seconds. Stir in cherry mixture and bring to boil. Add cream and simmer until reduced to sauce consistency, about 4 minutes. Season sauce to taste with salt and pepper. Slice duck breasts on diagonal and arrange on plates. Spoon sauce over duck.

# Duck Salad with Chutney Dressing

4 SERVINGS; CAN BE DOUBLED

The sweetness of duck and melon are irresistible in this colorful dish, which is also delicious when made with dark turkey meat or chicken breasts. Offer warm, buttery croissants with the salad, then splurge on apple strudel from the bakery — served à la mode, of course. (Pictured below.)

¾ cup peanut oil or vegetable oil
½ cup plus 1 tablespoon mango chutney
¼ cup plus 2 tablespoons white wine vinegar
1 tablespoon Dijon mustard
1 tablespoon soy sauce
1 tablespoon oriental sesame oil
¾ teaspoon dried crushed red pepper
2 large garlic cloves, chopped
6 boneless duck breast halves or 4 boneless chicken breast halves
2 tablespoons peanut oil or vegetable oil

2 cups cantaloupe chunks (about ¾-inch pieces)
1 cup thinly sliced celery
½ cup thinly sliced green onions
⅓ cup roasted salted cashews
Lettuce leaves

Puree first 8 ingredients in processor or blender. Season with salt and pepper. Generously salt and pepper duck pieces. Heat oil in heavy large skillet over medium-high heat. Cook duck, skin side down, until very brown and crisp, about 5 minutes. Turn and sauté duck until just cooked through, 5 minutes. Discard skin. Thinly slice duck across grain.

Combine duck, cantaloupe and celery in large bowl. Reserve 1 tablespoon green onions and add remainder to salad. Add cashews to salad. Toss with enough dressing to coat. Mound salad on lettuce. Sprinkle onions over. Serve, passing remaining dressing.

# SEAFOOD

When we were growing up, seafood at home usually meant frozen fish sticks or tuna salad on white. Unless you happened to live within a stone's throw of the seashore, fresh fish was hard to come by. And even if someone brought home a local catch, few people knew what to do with it.

Things sure have changed. Thanks to factors that range from jet-fast shipping to fish farming, a wide variety of high-quality fresh seafood is now available coast to coast, even in the most landlocked of areas. Supermarkets have begun to sell fresh fish and shellfish, though we still generally favor the small local purveyors who tend to have a better working knowledge of how to store and cook and serve seafood, and can also give us a better assurance of the freshness of the catch they're selling.

Every kind of fish and shellfish is quick-cooking. In fact, the greatest sin against seafood is, to our minds, overcooking the delicate flesh, which can turn juicy moistness into dry flakes in just minutes. That standard cooking rule, commonly called the Canadian Rule, is to measure the fish at its thickest point (including breading and stuffing), then allow 10 minutes of cooking time per inch of thickness. With a few exceptions, this rule works well whether you're poaching, frying, grilling, baking or broiling.

Almost all seafood is a relatively low-fat, high-quality source of protein. Years back, that and a low-calorie content encouraged us to try preparing fish and shellfish at home. But it was the quick-cooking, good-tasting results that made seafood a part of our everyday-cooking repertoire — and a favorite.

This varied collection of seafood recipes includes quick and contempo-

Grilled Tuna, Potato and Green Bean Salad (page 87)

rary versions of classic stews, such as Monkfish Cioppino (page 92) and Carolina Oyster Stew (page 113), along with such regional sandwich favorites as a New England Lobster Roll (page 108) and Hot Crab Salad Sandwiches (page 115). Some of our ideas were inspired by our experiences with international seafood cookery, including Shrimp and Snow Pea Paella (page 115) and Halibut Provençale (page 91). There are dishes here for simple weeknight suppers, such as Braised Cod and Golden Onions (page 89), along with others sophisticated — but still easy — enough to make for a Saturday-night dinner party, such as Salmon Steaks with Tomatillo-Apple Salsa (page 95).

Fish Soup with
Saffron and
Cream
(page 100)

The delicate texture and flavor of seafood is best complemented by light, seasonal side dishes, such as steamed broccoli or asparagus, a rice or orzo pilaf, and a salad with a simple vinaigrette. Chowders, soups and stews almost always go well with crusty bread or soup crackers. And for dessert, we like something citrusy after a seafood supper, maybe orange sherbet drizzled with anise liqueur or a slice of lemon meringue pie.

The wide variety and high quality of seafood available, coupled with its nutrition benefits and terrific taste, make fish and shellfish a mainstay on the menu of every time-conscious cook today.

## Grilled Tuna, Potato and Green Bean Salad

2 SERVINGS; CAN BE DOUBLED

Whole wheat breadsticks and sliced tomatoes make great accompaniments. Wedges of honeydew, cantaloupe and watermelon are a refreshing dessert. (Pictured on page 84.)

| | |
|---|---|
| 4 | tablespoons olive oil |
| 1½ | tablespoons tarragon vinegar |
| 1 | large shallot, chopped |
| 8 | ounces red-skinned potatoes, cut into ¾-inch pieces |
| 8 | ounces green beans, trimmed, halved |
| 1 | 8-ounce 1-inch-thick tuna steak, cut into 1-inch pieces |
| 2 | bamboo skewers, soaked in water 10 minutes |

Whisk 3 tablespoons oil and 1½ tablespoons vinegar to blend in large bowl. Add shallot; season with salt and pepper. Cook potatoes in medium pot of boiling salted water until almost tender, about 7 minutes. Add green beans and continue cooking until beans and potatoes are just tender, about 4 minutes longer. Drain vegetables. Add vegetables to dressing and toss to coat. *(Can be prepared up to 3 hours ahead. Cover and let stand at room temperature.)*

Prepare barbecue (medium-high heat) or preheat broiler. Thread half of tuna onto each skewer. Brush with remaining 1 tablespoon oil. Grill until just cooked through, turning occasionally, about 6 minutes. Spoon salad onto plates. Arrange tuna over salad and serve.

❧

## Salmon with Sesame Vegetables

2 SERVINGS; CAN BE DOUBLED

Oriental water noodles or linguine, cooked then tossed with a sauce of oil, rice vinegar and soy sauce makes an ideal partner. For a big finish, serve scoops of frozen lemon yogurt with brown sugar wafer cookies or chocolate-dipped fortune cookies.

| | |
|---|---|
| 2 | skinless 6-ounce salmon fillets |
| 2 | teaspoons oriental sesame oil |
| 4 | tablespoons (½ stick) unsalted butter |
| 1 | medium leek (white and pale green parts only), thinly sliced |
| 1 | medium carrot, thinly sliced on diagonal |
| 2 | teaspoons grated peeled fresh ginger |
| 1 | large garlic clove, minced |
| ¾ | cup dry white wine |
| ½ | cup bottled clam juice |
| | Toasted sesame seeds |

Brush both sides of salmon fillets with sesame oil. Season with salt and pepper. Sear salmon in heavy medium skillet over high heat until just cooked through, about 2 minutes per side. Transfer salmon to platter. Reduce heat to medium. Melt 1 tablespoon butter in same skillet. Add leek, carrot, ginger and garlic and sauté until carrot is just tender, about 4 minutes. Spoon vegetables over salmon, dividing evenly. Tent with aluminum foil. Add wine and clam juice to skillet and boil until liquids are reduced to glaze, about 10 minutes. Whisk in remaining 3 tablespoons butter. Spoon sauce over salmon fillets and vegetables. Sprinkle with toasted sesame seeds and serve.

# QUICK FISH AND CHIPS

2 SERVINGS; CAN BE DOUBLED

Frozen french fries make perfectly suitable "chips." Serve coleslaw alongside, then a plate of sliced apples or pears and shortbread cookies to round out the casual meal. (Pictured below.)

½ cup all purpose flour
½ cup flat English ale or beer
1 tablespoon malt vinegar or cider vinegar
½ teaspoon baking soda

Vegetable oil (for frying)
1 12-ounce ½-inch-thick cod fillet or orange roughy fillet, cut crosswise into 8 strips
Malt vinegar or cider vinegar

Whisk flour, ale, 1 tablespoon vinegar and baking soda in medium bowl until well blended. Season batter generously with salt and pepper. *(Can be made 2 hours ahead. Cover; let stand at room temperature.)*

Pour oil into heavy medium skillet to depth of ½ inch. Heat oil to 350°F. Pat fish dry with paper towels. Season fish with salt and pepper. Dip 4 fish strips into batter; let excess drain back into bowl. Fry fish until brown on both sides and just cooked through, about 3 minutes per side. Using slotted spoon, transfer fish to paper towels and let drain. Repeat dipping and frying with remaining 4 fish strips. Arrange fish on platter. Serve, passing vinegar separately.

# BRAISED COD AND GOLDEN ONIONS

2 SERVINGS; CAN BE DOUBLED

Team the cod with mashed sweet potatoes and buttered peas, then serve slices of carrot cake topped with vanilla ice cream to finish.

1½ tablespoons unsalted butter
1 large onion, thinly sliced
¼ teaspoon dried thyme, crumbled
1 bay leaf
2 5- to 6-ounce cod fillets
⅓ cup whipping cream
¼ cup dry white wine

Chopped fresh chives

Melt unsalted butter in heavy medium skillet over medium-high heat. Add sliced onion and cook until golden and soft, stirring frequently, about 12 minutes. Add dried thyme and bay leaf to skillet and cook until mixture is fragrant, about 1 minute. Season cod fillets with salt and pepper and place on top of onions. Add whipping cream and white wine and swirl skillet to blend liquids. Bring liquids to simmer. Reduce heat to medium-low. Cover skillet and braise cod fillets until just cooked through, about 7 minutes.

Using spatula as aid, transfer cod fillets to medium-size platter. Boil sauce until slightly thickened, about 1 minute. Season fish to taste with salt and pepper. Discard bay leaf. Spoon sauce over fish. Garnish with chopped fresh chives and serve.

# SWORDFISH STEAKS WITH MANGO SALSA

2 SERVINGS; CAN BE DOUBLED

Toss fresh spinach with marinated artichoke hearts and their marinade to begin. Serve a white and wild rice pilaf and sugar snap peas on the side, then offer rice pudding for a finale.

1 ripe mango, peeled, cut into small pieces
3 green onions, chopped
2 to 3 tablespoons chopped fresh cilantro
1 tablespoon fresh lemon juice
2 teaspoons chopped seeded fresh jalapeño chili

1 12-ounce swordfish steak (¾ inch thick), halved
½ tablespoon olive oil

Combine first 5 ingredients in bowl. Season with salt and pepper. Let stand at room temperature 10 minutes to 2 hours.

Preheat broiler or prepare barbecue. Brush both sides of fish with oil. Season with salt and pepper. Broil about 4 inches from heat source or grill until just cooked through, about 3 minutes per side.

Arrange fish on plates. Spoon salsa over and serve.

# Salmon Cakes with Lemon-Herb Mayonnaise

6 SERVINGS; CAN BE DOUBLED

Begin with bowls of gazpacho, made quickly by blending purchased fresh salsa with chopped bell pepper and cucumber. Potato salad is a good choice alongside the salmon cakes (which, by the way, are just as nice made with canned salmon if you don't have fresh), while strawberries and angel food cake would make a pretty dessert.

| | |
|---|---|
| 2 | cups loosely packed crumbled cooked salmon |
| ½ | cup cornflake crumbs |
| 2 | green onions, chopped |
| ¼ | cup finely chopped celery |
| ¼ | cup mayonnaise |
| 2 | tablespoons chopped fresh thyme or 2 teaspoons dried, crumbled |
| | Dash of Worcestershire sauce |
| 1 | large egg |
| ¾ | cup mayonnaise |
| 1 | tablespoon fresh lemon juice |
| 1 | tablespoon prepared horseradish |
| 2½ | teaspoons chopped fresh thyme or 1 teaspoon dried, crumbled |
| 2 | tablespoons (¼ stick) butter |

Combine first 7 ingredients in medium bowl and stir gently to blend. Season with salt and pepper. Mix in egg. Shape salmon mixture into 6 patties, about ¾ inch thick. Arrange on plate.

Combine ¾ cup mayonnaise, lemon juice, horseradish and 2½ teaspoons thyme in small bowl. Season with salt and pepper. *(Salmon cakes and sauce can be prepared 1 day ahead. Wrap and chill.)*

Melt butter in heavy large skillet over medium-low heat. Add salmon cakes and sauté until brown and cooked through, about 5 minutes per side. Transfer to platter. Serve with sauce.

# Peppery Panfried Catfish

4 SERVINGS; CAN BE DOUBLED

The crunchy cornmeal crust is great on other firm-fleshed white fish fillets, too. Serve red-cabbage coleslaw and french fries alongside. Offer vanilla pudding with raspberries for dessert.

| | |
|---|---|
| ¼ | cup plus 2 tablespoons yellow cornmeal |
| ¼ | cup plus 2 tablespoons all purpose flour |
| 1 | tablespoon grated lemon peel |
| ½ | teaspoon cayenne pepper |
| ⅔ | cup buttermilk |
| 4 | 6-ounce catfish fillets |
| 2 | tablespoons (¼ stick) butter |
| 1 | tablespoon vegetable oil |
| 1 | tablespoon minced fresh parsley |
| | Lemon wedges |

Combine cornmeal, flour, lemon peel and cayenne in shallow dish. Season with salt. Pour buttermilk into second shallow dish. Dip 1 fish fillet into buttermilk, then into cornmeal mixture, coating completely. Repeat process with remaining fish.

Melt butter with oil in heavy large skillet over medium-high heat. Add fish and cook until crust is golden brown and fish is cooked through, turning once, about 4 minutes per side. Transfer fish to platter. Sprinkle with minced parsley. Garnish with lemon wedges.

# HALIBUT PROVENÇALE

2 SERVINGS; CAN BE DOUBLED

Offer steamed and buttered new potatoes and baby zucchini with this dish, and apple brown betty for dessert. (Pictured above.)

2 plum tomatoes, seeded, chopped
3 tablespoons chopped brine-cured black olives (such as Kalamata)
2 teaspoons drained capers
1½ tablespoons olive oil
2 teaspoons fresh lemon juice

2 6- to 8-ounce halibut steaks or fillets (1 inch thick)

Combine tomatoes, olives, capers, 1 tablespoon olive oil and lemon juice in small bowl. Season to taste with salt and pepper *(Can be prepared 3 hours ahead. Let stand at room temperature.)*

Preheat oven to 425°F. Brush remaining ½ tablespoon oil over bottom of 9-inch pie dish or shallow pan. Season fish on both sides with pepper. Arrange in prepared dish. Spoon half of tomato mixture over each fish steak. Bake fish until just cooked through, about 15 minutes. Arrange fish on plates. Spoon pan juices over and serve.

# MONKFISH CIOPPINO

2 SERVINGS; CAN BE DOUBLED

Start this quickly prepared meal with a romaine and Belgian endive salad with vinaigrette dressing. Serve garlic toasts and some hearty red wine with the "stew," and then sliced oranges drizzled with Marsala to finish.
(Pictured at right.)

| 2 | tablespoons olive oil |
|---|---|
| 1 | small fennel bulb, trimmed, coarsely chopped, fennel fronds reserved |
| 1 | small green bell pepper, coarsely chopped |
| 1 | medium onion, thinly sliced |
| 2 | large garlic cloves, minced |
| 2 | teaspoons fennel seeds |
| 1 | 14½-ounce can Italian-style stewed tomatoes |
| 1 | 8-ounce bottle clam juice |
| 10 | to 12 ounces monkfish or sea bass fillet, cut into 1-inch pieces |

Heat olive oil in heavy large saucepan over medium-high heat. Add chopped fennel, chopped green pepper, sliced onion, minced garlic and fennel seeds. Cover pan and cook until vegetables are tender, stirring occasionally, about 5 minutes. Add stewed tomatoes and clam juice. Boil until mixture is slightly thickened, stirring occasionally, about 10 minutes. *(Stew can be prepared 1 day ahead. Cover tightly and refrigerate. Bring stew to simmer before continuing.)*

Add fish to stew. Simmer until fish is just cooked through, stirring occasionally, about 5 minutes. Season with salt and pepper. Transfer cioppino to large bowl. Chop reserved fennel fronds and sprinkle over.

# DILLED SEAFOOD EN PAPILLOTE

2 SERVINGS; CAN BE DOUBLED

Spread butter and horseradish on thin baguette rounds and top with baby shrimp for a nice opener. Boil tiny red potatoes and green beans to have alongside the seafood packets, and serve a pretty rhubarb dessert of your own design for the sweet.

| 8 | ounces skinless salmon fillet |
|---|---|
| 4 | ounces bay scallops |
| 3 | tablespoons thinly sliced green onion |
| 4 | teaspoons chopped fresh dill or 2 teaspoons dried dillweed |
| 2 | tablespoons fresh lemon juice |
| 4 | teaspoons butter |
| | Lemon wedges |

Preheat oven to 475°F. Cut two 16 x 12-inch pieces aluminum foil. Fold in half crosswise to make two 8 x 12-inch rectangles. Open foil on work surface. Set foil pieces aside.

Cut salmon crosswise into ½-inch-wide strips. Overlap half of salmon strips on one-half of each foil piece. Sprinkle scallops over. Season with salt and pepper. Sprinkle with green onion and dill, then drizzle with lemon juice and dot with butter. Fold other half of foil over fish. Fold in edges and pinch tightly to seal, making packages. Place on baking sheet. Bake until packages puff and seafood is just cooked through, about 8 minutes. Transfer packages to plates; garnish with lemon wedges. Cut open with small knife or scissors and serve.

# Trout Caprèse

2 SERVINGS; CAN BE DOUBLED

Here, the classic tomato, fresh mozzarella and basil salad becomes a flavorful topping for baked trout. Roasted, peppery potato wedges would be nice with the fish. After dinner, drizzle fresh or canned figs with marsala and serve with *biscotti*.

| | |
|---|---|
| 2 | 8- to 10-ounce fresh trout, butterflied, boned |
| 1 | cup diced seeded plum tomatoes |
| ¾ | cup diced fresh mozzarella cheese |
| ⅓ | cup chopped fresh basil |
| 2 | large garlic cloves, minced |
| 3 | tablespoons olive oil |
| 1 | tablespoon balsamic vinegar or red wine vinegar |

Preheat oven to 375°F. Brush baking sheet with oil. Lay fish on prepared sheet; open like books. Combine tomatoes, cheese, basil, garlic, 3 tablespoons oil and vinegar in small bowl. Season to taste with salt and pepper. Spoon salad over fish, spreading to cover completely. Bake until fish is just cooked through, about 15 minutes. Serve immediately.

# Sautéed Sole with Tomato-Caper Compote

4 SERVINGS; CAN BE DOUBLED

The lemony sauce is a delightful foil for sautéed fish of any type. Complete the easy dinner with boiled new potatoes, steamed asparagus spears and a purchased chocolate cake for dessert.

| | |
|---|---|
| ¾ | cup all purpose flour |
| ¾ | teaspoon salt |
| ¾ | teaspoon pepper |
| ¾ | cup milk |
| 1½ | pounds sole fillets |
| 6 | tablespoons olive oil |
| ¼ | cup (½ stick) butter |
| 1¼ | pounds ripe plum tomatoes, peeled, seeded, diced |
| 6 | tablespoons chopped fresh parsley |
| 3 | tablespoons fresh lemon juice |
| 1½ | tablespoons drained capers |
| | Lemon slices |
| | Additional capers |

Combine flour, salt and pepper in shallow dish. Pour milk into another shallow dish. Dip 1 fish fillet into milk to moisten, then into flour mixture, turning to coat completely. Place fillet on large sheet of waxed paper. Repeat procedure with remaining fillets.

Heat 3 tablespoons oil in heavy large skillet over medium-high heat. Add half of fish to skillet and sauté until light brown and cooked through, about 2 minutes per side. Transfer to platter. Repeat with remaining oil and fish fillets. Transfer fish to platter.

Melt butter in same skillet. Add tomatoes and simmer until tomatoes are soft, pressing and stirring occasionally, about 5 minutes. Mix in chopped parsley, lemon juice and 1½ tablespoons capers. Cook until thickened, stirring occasionally, about 5 minutes.

Spoon compote over fish. Garnish with lemon and capers.

## SALMON STEAKS WITH TOMATILLO-APPLE SALSA

4 SERVINGS; CAN BE DOUBLED

Buttered rice and sautéed zucchini are great side dishes for this tangy salmon recipe. Chocolate ice cream drizzled with coffee liqueur makes a perfect (and especially speedy) dessert. (Pictured above.)

5   fresh tomatillos,* husked, chopped (about 1 cup)
1   yellow or green bell pepper, seeded, chopped
1   small unpeeled Red Delicious apple, cored, chopped
½   cup chopped red onion
3   tablespoons chopped fresh cilantro
2   tablespoons olive oil
1   tablespoon fresh lemon juice
1   large jalapeño chili, seeded, minced
½   teaspoon salt

4   8-ounce salmon steaks (about 1 inch thick)
    Olive oil

Combine first 9 ingredients in medium bowl *(Can be prepared 3 hours ahead. Cover and let stand at room temperature.)*

Preheat broiler. Brush both sides of salmon with olive oil. Season with salt and pepper. Broil salmon 3 inches from heat source until just cooked through, about 5 minutes per side.

Arrange salmon on platter. Stir salsa well. Spoon some salsa over salmon. Pass extra salsa separately

*A green, tomato-like vegetable with a paper-thin husk. Available at Latin American markets, specialty foods stores and some supermarkets.*

## BROILED TROUT WITH TARRAGON AND LIME

2 SERVINGS; CAN BE DOUBLED

Accompany this elegant main course with roasted red potatoes and sautéed asparagus and green beans garnished with toasted almonds. Strawberry shortcake makes a nice dessert. (Pictured above.)

2   whole boned rainbow trout (8 to 10 ounces each)
1   tablespoon olive oil
1   fresh tarragon bunch
1   small fresh Italian parsley bunch
1   lime, thinly sliced

Lime wedges

Preheat broiler. Brush trout skin and cavities with oil. Season with salt and pepper. Chop enough tarragon to measure 2 teaspoons. Chop enough parsley to measure 2 tablespoons. Place half of chopped tarragon and parsley and 2 lime slices in each trout cavity. Fold trout closed. Spread remaining tarragon and parsley sprigs and lime slices on broiler pan as bed for trout. Top tarragon, parsley and lime with trout.

Broil trout about 4 inches from heat source until skin is brown, about 5 minutes. Using spatula, carefully turn trout over and broil until trout are cooked through, about 4 minutes. Arrange trout on platter. Garnish with lime wedges and serve.

# POACHED SALMON WITH SORREL CREAM

2 SERVINGS; CAN BE DOUBLED

Sorrel is a pleasantly tart green. Here, it is teamed with shallots and cream in a delicate sauce for the salmon. The dish would be good with white rice and steamed baby zucchini and yellow summer squash. Offer purchased chocolate truffles with cups of espresso to round out the meal.

| | |
|---|---|
| 2 | 6-ounce salmon fillets |
| 4 | thin lemon slices |
| 1 | tablespoon unsalted butter |
| 1 | tablespoon finely chopped shallots |
| ⅔ | cup thinly sliced sorrel or spinach (about 1 ounce) |
| ⅓ | cup whipping cream |
| ¼ | teaspoon grated lemon peel |

Season salmon fillets with salt and pepper. Place in heavy medium skillet. Cover salmon with water. Add lemon slices. Place skillet over medium heat and bring water just to simmer. Reduce heat to low. Cover and poach until just cooked through, about 8 minutes.

Meanwhile, melt butter in heavy small skillet over medium heat. Add shallots and sauté 30 seconds. Stir in sorrel, cream and lemon peel. Simmer gently until sauce is slightly thickened, about 2 minutes. Season to taste with salt and pepper.

Remove salmon from poaching liquid. Place salmon on serving plates and coat with sauce. Serve immediately.

# BAKED FISH IN MASHED POTATO CRUST

2 SERVINGS; CAN BE DOUBLED

We use scrod fillets when we make this dish to give it a New England flavor. Zucchini chunks simmered with stewed tomatoes and served with a basket of corn muffins can complete the main course, and purchased apple pie with wedges of Vermont cheddar could round out this Yankee menu.

| | |
|---|---|
| 1 | lemon |
| 1 | cup packed frozen mashed potatoes, thawed |
| 2 | large green onions, chopped |
| 1 | teaspoon dried thyme, crumbled |
| 2 | 5- to 6-ounce scrod fillets or other white fish fillets (such as orange roughy) |
| 2 | teaspoons butter |
| ½ | cup fresh French breadcrumbs |

Preheat oven to 450°F. Line small baking sheet with foil; lightly grease foil. Grate enough peel from lemon to measure 1 teaspoon. Mix potatoes, green onions, thyme and lemon peel in medium bowl until well blended. Season with salt and pepper. Arrange fish on prepared sheet. Season with salt and pepper; squeeze some lemon juice over. Spread half of potato mixture over each fillet, covering completely.

Melt butter in heavy small skillet over medium heat. Add breadcrumbs and toss until evenly coated. Spoon crumbs over potato crusts, dividing equally and pressing to adhere. Bake fish until just cooked through and potato crust and crumbs are beginning to brown, about 20 minutes. Serve immediately.

# GRILLED GROUPER WITH CANTALOUPE-LIME SALSA

2 SERVINGS; CAN BE DOUBLED

If you have time, cut up a combination of cantaloupe and honeydew to give the salsa even more color. Offer rice pilaf and sautéed sugar snap peas alongside the fish; then end by drizzling golden rum over chocolate frozen yogurt. (Pictured at left.)

½   cantaloupe, peeled, seeded, cubed (about 1 cup)
¼   cup chopped red onion
2   tablespoons chopped fresh cilantro
1½   tablespoons fresh lime juice
½   teaspoon grated lime peel
½   teaspoon ground pepper

10   to 12 ounces grouper fillets or other firm whitefish fillets
1   tablespoon oil

Prepare barbecue (medium-high heat) or preheat broiler. Mix first 6 ingredients in nonaluminum bowl. Season to taste with salt. Let stand at room temperature 15 minutes or refrigerate up to 2 hours.

Brush fish with oil. Season with salt and pepper. Grill fish until just cooked through, about 3 minutes per side. Transfer fish to plates. Spoon salsa over and serve immediately.

# HERBED PAUPIETTES OF SOLE

2 SERVINGS; CAN BE DOUBLED

Boiled small red potatoes, plus peas and carrots, could round out this sophisticated main course. Cookies and chocolate mousse are a nice finale.

6   small sole fillets (about 12 ounces total)
1½   teaspoons mixed dried herbs (such as tarragon, dillweed and thyme)
1½   tablespoons butter, melted
⅓   cup dry white wine
¼   cup fresh white breadcrumbs

Preheat oven to 450°F. Butter quiche dish or pie plate. Sprinkle fish with half of herbs. Season lightly with salt and pepper. Drizzle ½ tablespoon butter over. Starting at 1 short side, roll up fillets into cylinders. Arrange seam side down in prepared dish. Sprinkle with remaining herbs. Season with salt and pepper. Pour wine around fish. Mix breadcrumbs and ½ tablespoon butter in small bowl until crumbs are evenly coated. Sprinkle breadcrumbs over fish.

Bake until fish is cooked through and topping is crisp, about 15 minutes. Using slotted spoon, transfer fish to plates. Strain sauce into small skillet. Bring to simmer over low heat. Whisk in ½ tablespoon butter. Spoon sauce over fish and serve.

# FISH SOUP WITH SAFFRON AND CREAM

4 SERVINGS; CAN BE DOUBLED

This marvelous soup takes only minutes to prepare. Shrimp and another firm-fleshed fish make good substitutes for the scallops and sea bass. Asparagus vinaigrette, thick slices of French bread and a purchased lemon tart would round out this elegant dinner. (Pictured below.)

| | |
|---|---|
| 3 | tablespoons olive oil |
| 3 | medium carrots, peeled, chopped |
| 2 | leeks (white and pale green parts only), chopped |
| 2 | celery stalks, chopped |
| 1 | red bell pepper, chopped |
| 1 | bay leaf |
| | Generous pinch of saffron threads |
| 2 | cups dry white wine |
| 1½ | cups bottled clam juice |
| 1 | cup whipping cream |
| 1 | pound skinless sea bass filllet, cut into 1-inch pieces |
| 1 | pound sea scallops, cut in half crosswise |
| | Chopped fresh chives |

Heat oil in heavy large skillet over medium-high heat. Add carrots, leeks, celery, bell pepper, bay leaf and saffron to skillet and sauté 5 minutes. Add wine and clam juice to skillet and bring to boil. Reduce heat to medium and simmer 10 minutes. Add cream and simmer until vegetables are tender, about 5 minutes. Add fish and scallops to soup and simmer until just cooked through, about 3 minutes. Season to taste with salt and pepper. Remove bay leaf from soup. Ladle soup into large shallow bowls. Sprinkle with chopped chives and serve.

# Sole with Capers and Browned Butter

2 SERVINGS; CAN BE DOUBLED

Green beans and steamed baby potatoes go perfectly with this classic French "fast food." Follow the meal with a chocolate tart and cups of espresso.

|   |   |
|---|---|
| 1 | lemon, halved |
| ¼ | cup all purpose flour |
| ½ | teaspoon paprika |
| 4 | sole fillets (about 10 ounces) |
| 2½ | tablespoons butter |
| 1 | tablespoon drained capers |
| 1 | tablespoon chopped fresh parsley |

Thinly slice 1 lemon half and reserve. Squeeze juice from other lemon half and reserve 2½ teaspoons. Combine flour and paprika on plate. Season with salt and pepper. Coat fish with seasoned flour.

Melt 1½ tablespoons butter in heavy large skillet over medium-high heat. Add fish to skillet and sauté until just cooked through and light brown, about 2 minutes per side. Using large spatula, transfer fish to platter. Add remaining 1 tablespoon butter to same skillet and stir until light brown and fragrant, scraping up browned bits, about 2 minutes. Add reserved 2½ teaspoons lemon juice, capers and parsley and stir 10 seconds. Spoon sauce over fish, dividing evenly. Garnish with reserved lemon slices and serve immediately.

# Fish "Sticks" Veneziana

4 SERVINGS; CAN BE DOUBLED

For a soup course, gussy up canned minestrone with chopped tomatoes, fresh basil and grated Parmesan cheese. Serve these upscale fish sticks on angel hair pasta tossed with butter and garlic, and offer fruit tartlets to finish.

|   |   |
|---|---|
| 10 | paper-thin slices prosciutto or ham |
| 12 | ounces orange roughy fillets, cut crosswise into 10 strips |
| ⅓ | cup purchased pesto sauce |
| 10 | long slices peeled ripe pear |
| ½ | cup crumbled Gorgonzola cheese (about 2 ounces) |

Preheat oven to 375°F. Brush baking sheet lightly with olive oil. Lay prosciutto slice on work surface. Place fish strip close to one end. Spread ½ tablespoon pesto over fish. Lay pear slice over. Press ½ tablespoon cheese on pear. Fold prosciutto over and roll up to enclose fish and toppings (ends of roll will be open). Repeat with remaining prosciutto, fish, pesto, pear and cheese.

Arrange fish sticks on prepared baking sheet. Brush lightly with oil. Bake until fish is just cooked through, about 15 minutes. Serve.

# SALMON AND AVOCADO SCALOPPINE

2 SERVINGS; CAN BE DOUBLED

For a fancy appetizer before this sophisticated entrée, sprinkle tortilla chips (the kind made from flour tortillas) with chopped Brie and crumbled blue cheese and pop them in the microwave to melt. Orzo (rice-shaped pasta) is a good side dish; finish up with bowls of coffee ice cream drizzled with Kahlúa. (Pictured at right.)

| | |
|---|---|
| 6½ | tablespoons olive oil |
| 3 | tablespoons fresh lime juice |
| 1 | tablespoon minced lime peel |
| 1 | tablespoon minced seeded jalapeño chili |
| 1 | large avocado, peeled, halved lengthwise, pitted |
| 12 | ounces center-cut skinless salmon fillet, cut on deep diagonal into 10 thin slices |
| 2 | tablespoons chopped fresh cilantro |
| | Fresh lime wedges |

Preheat oven to 400°F. Line baking sheet with foil. Brush foil with ½ tablespoon olive oil. Whisk remaining 6 tablespoons oil, lime juice, lime peel and chili to blend in small bowl. Season dressing to taste with salt and pepper. Cut avocado halves lengthwise into thin slices. Arrange slices on plastic wrap and brush with dressing.

Arrange salmon on prepared baking sheet; brush with dressing. Bake salmon until just cooked through, about 2 minutes.

Alternate half of salmon scallops with half of avocado slices on each of 2 plates. Whisk chopped cilantro into dressing. Moisten salmon and avocado with a little dressing. Garnish with lime wedges and serve, passing remaining dressing separately.

❧

# MOROCCAN FISH

4 SERVINGS; CAN BE DOUBLED

This exotic dish would be good with couscous. If you'd like to add a vegetable to the meal, season eggplant and red bell pepper with cumin, drizzle with olive oil and broil until tender. Almond cookies and cups of tea scented with mint leaves would sum things up well.

| | |
|---|---|
| 2 | lemons, very thinly sliced |
| 4 | 6-ounce halibut fillets |
| | Olive oil |
| 2 | teaspoons ground cumin |
| ¼ | cup finely chopped onion |
| ¼ | cup finely chopped fresh cilantro |
| 24 | pimiento-stuffed green olives, chopped |

Preheat oven to 350°F. Place metal cooling rack on baking sheet. Place half of lemon slices on rack, arranging in 4 rows. Rub halibut with olive oil. Season both sides with cumin, salt and pepper. Place 1 fillet on each row of lemons. Sprinkle onion, cilantro, then olives evenly over halibut. Top with remaining lemon slices. Bake until halibut is just cooked through, about 20 minutes. Serve immediately.

# ROASTED FISH FILLETS WITH DILL AND SPINACH

4 SERVINGS; CAN BE DOUBLED

For a healthful, balanced supper, serve the fish with rice pilaf (add currants and cumin for seasoning), whole grain bread and a mixed green salad. Stay light for dessert, offering mixed fresh berries and low-fat frozen yogurt.

Nonstick vegetable oil spray
4   6-ounce skinless fish fillets (such as orange roughy, snapper or flounder)
1   tablespoon fresh lemon juice
4   teaspoons Dijon mustard
8   tablespoons finely chopped fresh dill or 2 tablespoons dried dillweed

1   teaspoon olive oil
2   10-ounce packages fresh spinach leaves, stems trimmed, rinsed, drained
1   garlic clove, minced
1   lemon, quartered lengthwise

Preheat oven to 450°F. Spray glass baking dish with nonstick vegetable oil spray. Arrange fish fillets in dish and sprinkle with 1 table-spoon fresh lemon juice. Spread 1 teaspoon Dijon mustard over each filet. Sprinkle fish with 7 tablespoons chopped dill. Bake until fish fillets are just cooked through, about 10 minutes.

Meanwhile, heat olive oil in large nonstick skillet over medium heat. Add spinach and minced garlic and stir just until spinach is wilted, about 3 minutes. Using tongs, transfer spinach to serving platter, leaving pan juices behind; top with fish fillets. Garnish with remaining 1 table-spoon chopped dill and lemon wedges.

# GRILLED TUNA WITH ROSEMARY BUTTER

2 SERVINGS; CAN BE DOUBLED

Start this elegant meal with steamed artichokes, then accompany the tuna with boiled red-skinned potatoes and a salad of mixed lettuces. A strawberry tart would be a lovely conclusion.

1½  tablespoons butter, room temperature
2   teaspoons chopped fresh rosemary or ¾ teaspoon dried, crumbled
1   teaspoon finely chopped fresh chives or green onions
1   teaspoon grated lemon peel

1   tablespoon fresh lemon juice
1   tablespoon olive oil
2   6-ounce tuna steaks (¾ to 1 inch thick)

Mix 1½ tablespoons butter, 1 teaspoon rosemary, chopped chives and grated lemon peel in small bowl. Season to taste with salt and pepper. *(Can be prepared 1 day ahead. Cover and refrigerate.)*

Prepare barbecue (medium-high heat) or preheat broiler. Combine lemon juice, oil and remaining 1 teaspoon rosemary in shallow baking dish. Sprinkle tuna on both sides with salt and pepper. Add to marinade, turning to coat. Let stand 15 minutes, turning twice.

Remove tuna from marinade; grill or broil tuna until just cooked through, about 4 minutes per side. Transfer to plate. Top with rosemary butter. Serve tuna immediately.

# CORNMEAL-CRUSTED CATFISH ON MIXED GREENS

2 SERVINGS; CAN BE DOUBLED

Serve green peas and french fries with the fish, then wrap things up with a purchased pecan pie.
(Pictured below.)

¼ cup yellow cornmeal
10 to 12 ounces catfish fillets, cut into 1-inch pieces
2½ tablespoons vegetable oil
2 tablespoons fresh lemon juice
1½ teaspoons honey
1½ teaspoons Dijon mustard
½ teaspoon grated lemon peel

3 cups mixed lettuces or mesclun
¼ cup thinly sliced sweet onion (such as Vidalia) or red onion

Place cornmeal in large bowl. Season with salt and pepper. Rinse catfish under cold water and shake off excess (do not pat dry). Toss fish in cornmeal mixture until well coated. Heat 2 tablespoons oil in large nonstick skillet over medium-high heat. Add catfish and cook until golden brown and cooked through, turning occasionally, about 6 minutes. Transfer to paper towels and drain. Add ½ tablespoon oil, lemon juice, honey, mustard and lemon peel to skillet and whisk until combined, about 30 seconds. Remove from heat.

Combine lettuces and onion in bowl. Add warm dressing and toss. Divide between 2 plates. Top with fish.

# SWORDFISH WITH WATERCRESS AND BACON TOPPING

2 SERVINGS; CAN BE DOUBLED

Dress up a simple piece of baked swordfish by topping it with this warm watercress salad and serving it on a large crouton of toasted country bread. Mashed butternut squash makes a deliciously different side dish, while purchased cherry strudel would be a good choice for dessert.
(Pictured at left.)

2   slices bacon
2   6- to 7-ounce ¾-inch-thick swordfish steaks

⅓   cup diced red bell pepper
⅓   cup chopped shallots
1   tablespoon olive oil
2   teaspoons Dijon mustard
1   teaspoon balsamic vinegar or red wine vinegar
1   large bunch watercress, stems trimmed

Preheat oven to 375°F. Cook bacon in heavy large skillet over medium heat until brown and crisp. Transfer bacon to paper towel and drain. Crumble bacon and reserve. Arrange swordfish on greased baking sheet; brush lightly with bacon drippings. Season with pepper. Bake swordfish until just cooked through, about 15 minutes.

Meanwhile, add red pepper, shallots and olive oil to bacon drippings in same skillet and sauté over medium heat until slightly soft, about 3 minutes. Blend in mustard and vinegar. Add watercress and toss until wilted and coated with dressing, about 2 minutes. Season watercress mixture with salt and pepper. Transfer swordfish to plates. Divide watercress topping between fish. Sprinkle with bacon and serve.

# BAKED HALIBUT WITH LEMON-PEPPER CRUST

2 SERVINGS; CAN BE DOUBLED

Scalloped potatoes and stewed tomatoes cooked with zucchini chunks are nice accompaniments; chocolate pudding is a delectable dessert.

2   slices firm white bread, crusts trimmed
⅓   cup finely chopped fresh parsley
2   teaspoons minced lemon peel
¾   teaspoon coarsely ground black pepper
2   6- to 7-ounce halibut fillets (1 inch thick)
2   tablespoons (¼ stick) unsalted butter, melted
    Lemon wedges

Preheat oven to 450°F. Lightly grease small baking sheet. Grind bread in processor to fine crumbs. Add parsley, lemon peel and pepper and combine; season with salt. Transfer crumb mixture to shallow soup bowl. Brush fish with butter. Press fish into crumbs, coating completely. Arrange fish on prepared baking sheet. Press any remaining crumbs onto top of fish. Bake until crumb coating is golden brown and fish is just cooked through, about 10 minutes. Serve with lemon wedges.

# GARLIC SHRIMP WITH SHERRY SAUCE

2 SERVINGS; CAN BE DOUBLED

White rice is great for catching the sauce, and steamed broad beans or lima beans add color. Brandy over chocolate ice cream ends the meal nicely.

½ cup dry Sherry
5 tablespoons olive oil
2 tablespoons fresh lemon juice
6 garlic cloves, minced
⅛ to ¼ teaspoon cayenne pepper
3 tablespoons chopped fresh parsley

12 ounces large uncooked shrimp, peeled, deveined

Boil Sherry, 1 tablespoon oil, lemon juice, garlic and cayenne pepper in heavy small saucepan until reduced to ¼ cup, about 7 minutes. Transfer mixture to blender. With machine running, gradually add 3 tablespoons oil and blend until smooth sauce forms. Season to taste with salt and pepper. Add parsley and blend in, using on/off turns.

Heat remaining 1 tablespoon oil in heavy medium skillet over high heat. Add shrimp and sauté until just cooked through, about 3 minutes. Divide shrimp between plates. Pour sauce over.

# NEW ENGLAND LOBSTER ROLL

2 SERVINGS; CAN BE DOUBLED

Curry makes a nice (if nontraditional) accent. Partner the sandwich with corn on the cob, then serve some purchased blueberry turnovers for dessert.

⅓ cup regular or reduced-calorie mayonnaise
1 green onion, chopped
1 teaspoon curry powder
Pinch of cayenne pepper
1½ cups (about 10 ounces) diced cooked lobster or shrimp
⅓ cup finely chopped celery

2 hot dog buns or French rolls
1 tablespoon butter, room temperature
4 Boston lettuce leaves

Combine mayonnaise, green onion, curry powder and cayenne pepper in medium bowl. Add lobster and celery and blend well. Season with salt and pepper. *(Can be prepared 3 hours ahead. Cover and chill.)*

Open buns and spread cut surfaces lightly with butter. Heat heavy large skillet over medium heat. Place buns buttered sides down in skillet and fry until golden brown. Remove from skillet. Place 2 lettuce leaves in each bun. Mound half of filling in each. Fold buns gently to enclose filling and serve sandwiches warm.

# SPICY MUSSELS STEAMED IN WHITE WINE

2 SERVINGS; CAN BE DOUBLED

Slices of pear wrapped in prosciutto are an elegant starter, and crusty bread is great for soaking up the mussel broth. Spumoni ice cream and *amaretti* cookies would be an appropriate finish to this Italian-themed meal.
(Pictured below.)

¼ cup olive oil
¾ cup coarsely chopped onion
4 anchovy fillets, chopped
3 large garlic cloves, chopped
¼ teaspoon dried crushed red pepper

2½ pounds fresh mussels, scrubbed, debearded
1 cup dry white wine
⅓ cup chopped parsley

Heat olive oil in heavy medium skillet over medium heat. Add chopped onion and sauté until tender, about 6 minutes. Add anchovies, garlic and crushed pepper and sauté 5 minutes, mashing anchovies to paste with back of fork. *(Onion mixture can be prepared up to 1 hour ahead. Let stand at room temperature.)*

Combine mussels and wine in heavy large saucepan or Dutch oven; bring to boil over high heat. Cover pan; boil until mussels open, 7 minutes. Remove from heat. Using tongs, transfer mussels to 2 large soup bowls, discarding any mussels that do not open. Strain mussel cooking liquid into skillet with onion. Boil mixture over high heat until slightly reduced, 2 minutes. Mix in parsley. Ladle broth over mussels.

# MIXED SEAFOOD IN CREAMY CURRY SAUCE

4 SERVINGS; CAN BE DOUBLED

For quick condiments to serve with this curry, try raisins, chopped green onions, shredded coconut and mango chutney. Rice is a good go-with, as is beer. End with scoops of frozen yogurt.
(Pictured at right.)

| | |
|---|---|
| ¼ | cup (½ stick) unsalted butter |
| 1 | ½-pound halibut fillet, cut into ¾-inch cubes |
| ½ | pound bay scallops |
| ½ | pound uncooked shrimp, peeled, deveined |
| 1 | medium onion, chopped |
| 1 | small red bell pepper, chopped |
| 1 | garlic clove, minced |
| 1 | teaspoon curry powder |
| ½ | cup bottled clam juice |
| ½ | cup whipping cream |
| 1½ | ounces cream cheese |
| 1 | tablespoon (or more) fresh lemon juice |

Melt butter in heavy large skillet over high heat. Add halibut, scallops and shrimp and sauté until partially cooked, about 3 minutes. Using slotted spoon, transfer seafood to bowl. Boil juices in skillet until almost reduced to glaze, stirring occasionally, about 4 minutes. Add onion, bell pepper and garlic to skillet. Sauté until light brown, about 3 minutes. Sprinkle curry powder over and stir 30 seconds. Add clam juice, cream, cream cheese and 1 tablespoon lemon juice. Boil until mixture is reduced to 1½ cups, stirring frequently, about 10 minutes. Return seafood and any collected juices to skillet and simmer until cooked through. Season with salt, pepper and lemon juice.

# SAUTÉED SEA SCALLOPS WITH LEMON DILL SAUCE

2 SERVINGS; CAN BE DOUBLED

Steamed spinach and rice with tomato and onion make tasty side dishes. Top off this light meal with the best chocolate mousse cake you can buy.
(Pictured on page 182.)

| | |
|---|---|
| ¼ | cup all purpose flour |
| ½ | pound sea scallops |
| 5 | tablespoons butter |
| ½ | cup dry white wine |
| 1 | tablespoon chopped fresh dill or 1 teaspoon dried dillweed |
| 1 | teaspoon grated lemon peel |
| | Lemon wedges |
| | Fresh dill sprigs (optional) |

Season flour with salt and pepper. Dredge scallops in flour mixture. Shake off excess. Melt 2 tablespoons butter in heavy medium skillet over high heat. Add scallops and sauté until cooked through, turning occasionally, about 3 minutes. Using tongs, transfer scallops to platter. Cover platter with foil to keep scallops warm.

Add wine to same skillet. Bring to boil, scraping up browned bits. Boil until reduced to 3 tablespoons, about 3 minutes. Add dill and lemon peel. Reduce heat to very low. Add remaining 3 tablespoons butter and whisk just until melted. Season sauce to taste with salt and pepper. Spoon sauce over scallops. Garnish with lemon wedges and dill sprigs if desired and serve immediately.

# CLASSIC CRAB CAKES

2 SERVINGS; CAN BE DOUBLED

Lemon wedges and hot pepper sauce are the ideal condiments, with steamed green beans and potato salad to round out the meal. Make or buy a blueberry cobbler for dessert.
(Pictured below with the Black-eyed Pea and Feta Salad from page 164.)

⅓ cup reduced-calorie mayonnaise
¾ teaspoon Old Bay or other seafood seasoning
6 ounces crabmeat, picked over, patted dry (about 1 cup packed)
⅔ cup saltine cracker crumbs (about 16 crackers)
¼ cup minced green onions
¼ cup minced red bell pepper

1 tablespoon vegetable oil

Mix mayonnaise and seasoning in medium bowl. Add crabmeat, ⅓ cup cracker crumbs, green onions and bell pepper. Mix carefully to avoid breaking up crabmeat. Form mixture into four ½-inch-thick patties. Place remaining ⅓ cup cracker crumbs in shallow bowl. Press crab cakes into crumbs, coating completely. (*Can be prepared 3 hours ahead. Cover and refrigerate.*)

Heat oil in heavy nonstick skillet over medium heat. Fry cakes until brown and crisp, about 6 minutes per side. Serve immediately.

# CAROLINA OYSTER STEW

2 SERVINGS; CAN BE DOUBLED

Substituting milk for all or part of the half and half will result in a lighter soup. Oyster crackers are nice alongside. Begin with a spinach and romaine salad, and finish with apple pie.

2 tablespoons (¼ stick) butter
1 large celery stalk with leafy tops, thinly sliced
2 tablespoons all purpose flour
1 cup thinly sliced green onions
3 cups half and half or milk
2 8-ounce jars oysters, drained, liquid reserved
1 large potato, peeled, cut into ¼-inch cubes
2 teaspoons Worcestershire sauce

Hot pepper sauce (such as Tabasco)

Melt 2 tablespoons butter in heavy medium saucepan over medium heat. Add sliced celery and sauté until beginning to soften, about 3 minutes. Mix in flour, then ½ cup sliced green onions and stir 2 minutes. Gradually mix in half and half and reserved oyster liquid. Add potato. Stir until soup comes to boil and thickens. Reduce heat to low and simmer until potato is tender, about 8 minutes. Add oysters and Worcestershire sauce and simmer until edges of oysters begin to curl, about 3 minutes. Season to taste with salt and pepper.

Ladle soup into bowls. Garnish with remaining green onions and serve, passing hot pepper sauce separately.

# PRAWNS WITH ROMESCO SAUCE

2 SERVINGS; CAN BE DOUBLED

You can steam, grill, boil or broil the shrimp or, even easier, buy them already cooked. Saffron rice and mixed greens tossed with olives, red onion slices and a garlicky olive oil dressing are good side dishes. Crisp cookies and sliced oranges sprinkled with sweet Sherry round out the Spanish-inspired menu.

2 tablespoons slivered almonds
1 thin slice French bread (about 4 x 3 x ¼-inch)
1 large garlic clove
1 7-ounce jar roasted red peppers, drained
2 tablespoons olive oil
1 tablespoon Sherry wine vinegar or red wine vinegar
¼ teaspoon cayenne pepper

8 cooked jumbo shrimp (8 to 10 ounces), peeled, deveined

Stir almonds in heavy small skillet over medium heat until golden, about 3 minutes. Transfer almonds to processor. Place bread in same skillet and cook until lightly toasted, about 1 minute per side. Tear bread into pieces and add to processor. With machine running, drop garlic through feed tube and process until almonds and garlic are finely chopped. Add peppers, oil, vinegar and cayenne and process until mixture is consistency of thick mayonnaise, scraping down sides of bowl occasionally. *(Can be prepared 1 day ahead. Cover and refrigerate.)*

Arrange shrimp on plates. Spoon sauce over and serve.

## SHRIMP AND SNOW PEA PAELLA

2 SERVINGS; CAN BE DOUBLED

With paella as the centerpiece dish of a dinner, all that you need as complements are a basket of good bread and a green salad with red onions and avocado. A rich, creamy flan will end the meal on a suitably Spanish note.
(Pictured at left.)

½ cup (or more) canned low-salt chicken broth
⅛ teaspoon powdered saffron
6 ounces fully cooked sausage (such as kielbasa), diced
⅔ cup long-grain white rice
1 8-ounce bottle clam juice

3 ounces snow peas (about 1 cup), trimmed, cut in half diagonally
9 ounces large uncooked shrimp, peeled, deveined

Heat ½ cup broth in heavy small saucepan over medium heat just until warm. Stir in saffron. Sauté sausage in heavy medium skillet over medium-high heat until brown, about 2 minutes. Add rice to same skillet and stir to coat with sausage drippings. Add saffron mixture and clam juice. Bring to boil. Reduce heat to medium-low, cover skillet and simmer rice mixture for 15 minutes.

Add snow peas and shrimp to skillet, pushing shrimp into rice. Add more broth if rice seems dry. Cover and cook until shrimp are cooked through and rice is tender, stirring once, about 8 minutes. Season paella to taste with salt and pepper and serve.

## HOT CRAB SALAD SANDWICHES

2 SERVINGS; CAN BE DOUBLED

Start with tomato soup, and serve a watercress and mixed green salad with mustard vinaigrette alongside the sandwich. Conclude the meal with chocolate-walnut brownies.

1 6-ounce can fancy lump crabmeat, drained, picked over
1 cup packed shredded Muenster cheese (about 4 ounces)
4 tablespoons chopped green onions
2 tablespoons mayonnaise
1 teaspoon Worcestershire sauce

2 English muffins, split

Combine crabmeat, ½ cup Muenster cheese, 3 tablespoons green onions, mayonnaise and Worcestershire sauce in medium bowl and stir to blend. Season filling with pepper.

Preheat broiler. Arrange muffin halves, split side up, on baking sheet. Broil just until beginning to color, about 1 minute. Mound ¼ of crabmeat mixture on each muffin half. Top with remaining cheese and remaining green onions, dividing evenly. Broil until filling is heated through and cheese melts, watching closely, about 2 minutes.

# CHESAPEAKE BAY CRAB SOUP

4 SERVINGS; CAN BE DOUBLED

If you can get fresh Maryland lump crabmeat, do so — this sublime soup is worth it. Serve with baking powder biscuits and a romaine salad with creamy vinaigrette. Lemon pound cake makes an excellent dessert.

| | |
|---|---|
| 2 | tablespoons olive oil |
| 1 | medium onion, chopped |
| 1 | carrot, peeled, chopped |
| 1 | 16-ounce can Italian plum tomatoes |
| 2 | cups canned chicken broth |
| 1 | cup water |
| 1 | cup bottled clam juice |
| ½ | cup dry white wine |
| 1 | large potato, cut into ½-inch pieces |
| 2 | teaspoons Worcestershire sauce |
| 1½ | teaspoons Old Bay Seasoning |
| 1 | cup frozen peas |
| 12 | ounces fresh lump crabmeat, or frozen, thawed, undrained, picked over |
| 2 | tablespoons chopped fresh parsley |
| ½ | teaspoon hot pepper sauce (such as Tabasco) |

Heat oil in heavy large saucepan over medium heat. Add onion and carrot and cook until vegetables begin to soften, stirring occasionally, about 5 minutes. Add tomatoes with their liquid; break up tomatoes. Add chicken broth, water, clam juice, wine, potato, Worcestershire sauce and Old Bay Seasoning. Bring to boil; reduce heat, cover and simmer until potatoes are tender, about 12 minutes.

Add peas to soup and simmer 2 minutes. Add crabmeat, parsley and hot pepper sauce. Simmer until crabmeat is heated through, about 1 minute. Season with salt and pepper and serve.

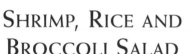

# SHRIMP, RICE AND BROCCOLI SALAD

2 SERVINGS; CAN BE DOUBLED

This recipe makes the most of leftover rice — either white or brown. And if you also have some leftover cooked broccoli in the refrigerator, then, you're really on your way here. Egg rolls are a good way to get started, with chocolate-dipped fortune cookies for dessert.

| | |
|---|---|
| ¼ | cup rice wine vinegar |
| 2 | tablespoons oriental sesame oil |
| 2 | tablespoons vegetable oil |
| 1½ | tablespoons soy sauce |
| 1 | tablespoon minced peeled fresh ginger |
| 2½ | cups cooked long-grain white rice or brown rice, room temperature |
| 2 | cups cooked broccoli florets |
| 1 | red bell pepper, coarsely chopped |
| 8 | ounces cooked peeled shrimp |

Whisk first 5 ingredients in small bowl to blend. Season to taste with salt and pepper. Combine rice, broccoli and bell pepper in medium bowl. Toss with half of dressing. Divide rice mixture between 2 plates. Arrange shrimp atop salads. Drizzle remaining dressing over.

## SHRIMP AND VEGETABLE BROCHETTES

2 SERVINGS; CAN BE DOUBLED

A salad of mixed lettuces and some orzo (rice-shaped pasta) tossed with chopped mint are the perfect accompaniments to these kebabs. Complete the meal with peach pie. (Pictured above.)

| | |
|---|---|
| 5 | tablespoons olive oil |
| 2½ | tablespoons fresh lemon juice |
| 1 | tablespoon Dijon mustard |
| ¾ | teaspoon grated lemon peel |
| 12 | uncooked large shrimp, peeled, deveined |
| 4 | 10- to 12-inch-long bamboo skewers, soaked in water 10 minutes |
| 1 | medium zucchini, trimmed, cut into ½-inch-thick rounds |
| 1 | red bell pepper, cut into 1½-inch squares |
| 6 | green onions, trimmed |

In small bowl, whisk olive oil, lemon juice, mustard and grated lemon peel until blended. Season marinade to taste with salt and pepper. *(Can be made 1 day ahead. Cover and let stand at room temperature.)*

Prepare barbecue (medium-high heat). Add shrimp to marinade; toss. Marinate shrimp 10 minutes. Drain shrimp; transfer marinade to saucepan and bring to boil. Thread 6 shrimp on each of 2 skewers. Alternate zucchini and bell peppers on 2 remaining skewers.

Grill vegetable and shrimp skewers and green onions until just cooked through, turning occasionally and basting with marinade, about 12 minutes for vegetables, 4 minutes for shrimp and 3 minutes for green onions. Remove skewers from grill and serve.

# BEEF, VEAL, LAMB, PORK

When it's maximum impact we're after, with minimum effort, we tend to turn to beef, veal, lamb or pork. Whether it's ground meats, small chops, cutlets or steaks (all of them easily prepared in under 30 minutes), meat always offers real "bang for the buck."

These days, with more and more quick-cooking lean and boneless cuts available, our meat options are wider than ever. The only trick in preparing them? Making sure they don't get overcooked, which causes them to dry out, lose flavor and turn the texture of shoe leather. Test for doneness frequently and regulate the heat carefully and you'll be ensured of success.

Thank goodness for good old-fashioned hamburgers, a favorite (not to mention a savior on particularly harried nights) we don't need to tell you how to make. But you might like some ideas for jazzing up ground beef, so we've included recipes for flavorful Sloppy Joes (page 132) and Texas Beef Tacos (page 129). Other cuts, steak in particular, can still be the best choice when that special guest (maybe the boss, with her boyfriend) comes to dinner. For your consideration: elegant but easy Filet Mignons with Red Pepper Sauce (page 127) or sophisticated Steaks in Sherried Mushroom Sauce (page 124).

The delicate, rather shy flavor of veal tends to take on some of the personality of more assertive partners, occasionally creating marriages made in heaven. Delicious partnerships here include Veal Chops with Tomato Relish (page 136), Veal Scallops with Cranberry-Citrus Compote (page 134) and Veal Saltimbocca (page 137), our take on that classic — and delicious — layering of meat, cheese, prosciutto and herbs.

Grilled Steak
with Southwest
Relish (page 121)

Lamb, on the other hand, has a bold flavor uniquely its own. Some like it cooked very simply, paired with clean, straightforward seasonings, as in Roast Rack of Lamb with Parsleyed Crumbs (page 145). Others prefer their lamb prepared with equally assertive ingredients. For them we've included zesty Spiced Lamb Burgers (page 141), Lamb Chops on Warm Lentil Salad (page 140) and exotically seasoned Lamb Kebabs with Peanut Sauce (page 147).

Pork Chops
Braised with
Cider and Apples
(page 152)

There are any number of ways to prepare pork (the "other white meat") in half an hour, what with all the cuts available now, including boneless tenderloins, chops and cutlets. By way of example, try such seductive dishes as peppery Pork Tenderloin with Lemon and Fennel (page 152), autumnal Pork Chops Braised with Cider and Apples (page 152) and ultra-quick Pork Cutlets with Mustard-Maple Sauce (page 151).

Pork also appears in the guise of ham and all kinds of savory sausages. Ever-popular ham stars in Maple Mustard-glazed Ham Steak (page 149). Well-seasoned sausages form the basis of many wonderful dishes here, including Sausages and White Beans on Arugula (page 154), Sausage Ratatouille (page 155) and spicy Chorizo, Pepper and Onion Sandwiches (page 155).

Whether it's a special occasion or just an ordinary weeknight, meat, in its infinite variety, can fill just about any bill.

# GRILLED STEAK WITH SOUTHWEST RELISH

2 SERVINGS; CAN BE DOUBLED

Sautéed summer squash and grilled slices of thickly cut boiled potatoes round out this meal nicely. Sugared berries or sliced fresh plums over lemon sherbet would make a cool finale. (Pictured on page 118.)

| | |
|---|---|
| 1 | cup chopped seeded tomato |
| ½ | cup diced yellow or green bell pepper |
| 3 | tablespoons minced fresh cilantro |
| 2½ | tablespoons vegetable oil |
| 2 | teaspoons minced canned pickled jalapeños |
| 1½ | teaspoons pickled jalapeño liquid |
| ½ | teaspoon ground cumin |
| 2 | ¾-inch-thick New York strip steaks (about 8 ounces each) |

Combine first 7 ingredients in small bowl. Season relish to taste with salt and pepper. *(Relish can be prepared 3 hours ahead. Cover with plastic wrap and let stand at room temperature.)*

Prepare barbecue (medium-high heat). Season steaks with salt and pepper. Grill to desired doneness, about 4 minutes per side for medium-rare. Arrange steaks on plates. Spoon relish over and serve.

# CONTEMPORARY SWISS STEAK

4 SERVINGS; CAN BE DOUBLED

Serve with green beans and mashed potatoes, followed by freshly baked pears and whipped cream.

| | |
|---|---|
| 3 | tablespoons all purpose flour |
| ¼ | teaspoon salt |
| ¼ | teaspoon pepper |
| 1 | pound cubed steak, cut into 4 pieces |
| 4 | tablespoons vegetable oil |
| 1 | large onion, thinly sliced |
| 1 | large celery stalk, sliced |
| 1 | medium carrot, very thinly sliced |
| 1 | large garlic clove, minced |
| 1 | 14½-ounce can stewed tomatoes |
| ½ | cup dry red wine |
| 1 | teaspoon dried oregano, crumbled |
| 1 | teaspoon dried savory, crumbled |
| 2 | tablespoons chopped fresh parsley |

Combine flour, salt and pepper in shallow dish. Dredge both sides of steak pieces lightly in flour mixture. Reserve remaining flour.

Heat 2 tablespoons oil in heavy large skillet over high heat. Cook steak until brown, 2 minutes per side. Transfer to plate.

Add remaining 2 tablespoons oil to skillet. Reduce heat to medium. Add onion, celery and carrot. Cover skillet and cook until vegetables are tender, stirring occasionally, about 8 minutes. Add garlic and reserved flour and cook 1 minute, stirring constantly. Add stewed tomatoes with their liquid, wine, oregano and savory. Return steaks and any accumulated juices to skillet, spooning vegetables over. Bring to simmer. Reduce heat to low. Cover skillet and cook steaks until tender, about 10 minutes. Uncover skillet and simmer 2 minutes to thicken gravy. Season with salt and pepper. Transfer to platter. Garnish with parsley.

# GRILLED ROAST BEEF AND STILTON SANDWICHES

4 SERVINGS; CAN BE DOUBLED

Even the English would approve of serving these delicious sandwiches with mounds of crisp french fries and some malt vinegar (or ketchup, if you must) for dipping. Ale to drink, of course. (Pictured below.)

| | |
|---|---|
| 1 | cup crumbled Stilton cheese |
| 2 | tablespoons mayonnaise |
| 1 | tablespoon prepared horseradish |
| 8 | 3 x 5-inch sourdough bread slices |
| 1 | pound thinly sliced roast beef |
| ½ | red onion, thinly sliced |
| 1 | bunch arugula, stems trimmed |
| 2 | tablespoons (¼ stick) butter |

Mash first 3 ingredients in small bowl until almost smooth. Place bread on work surface and spread mixture on 1 side of each slice. Top each of 4 bread slices with ¼ of beef, then onion and arugula. Season with pepper. Top with remaining bread, cheese side down.

Melt butter in heavy large skillet over medium-high heat. Add sandwiches and cook until golden, about 2 minutes per side. Serve hot.

# Beef and Chicken Burritos

4 SERVINGS; CAN BE DOUBLED

Purchased salsa is part of the filling here; you can serve more salsa, chopped fresh cilantro and sour cream as condiments. To begin the meal, heat a can of refried beans, stir in some shredded hot pepper Jack cheese and offer with chips and jicama sticks. Afterwards, have cookies and glasses of lemonade.

4   10-inch (burrito-size) flour tortillas
2   tablespoons olive oil
1   onion, halved, thinly sliced
1   green bell pepper, thinly sliced
2   teaspoons chili powder
⅛   teaspoon cayenne pepper
2   skinless boneless chicken breast halves, sliced crosswise into ½-inch-thick strips
2   large garlic cloves, chopped
1   8-ounce top sirloin steak or tenderloin steak, sliced crosswise into ¼-inch-thick strips
½   cup mild thick bottled salsa

Preheat oven to 350°F. Wrap tortillas in aluminum foil and place in oven to heat through, about 10 minutes.

Heat oil in heavy large skillet over medium-high heat. Add onion, bell pepper, chili powder and cayenne and sauté until vegetables begin to soften, about 3 minutes. Add chicken and garlic and stir 3 minutes. Add beef and stir until just cooked through, about 3 minutes. Mix in salsa. Season filling to taste with salt and pepper.

Spoon ¼ of filling in center of each tortilla. Roll sides of tortilla over filling to enclose completely and serve.

~

# Szechuan Steak with Port-Ginger Sauce

2 SERVINGS; CAN BE DOUBLED

A take-out order of won ton soup would make a suitable first course for this Asian-themed dish, which you might accompany with steamed rice and broccoli. Green tea and fortune cookies (from that same Chinese restaurant) would be good after dinner.

1½   tablespoons Szechuan peppercorns
2    teaspoons drained green peppercorns in brine
2    6-ounce beef tenderloin steaks

1    teaspoon vegetable oil
1    cup ruby Port
¼    cup minced shallots
1½   tablespoons finely chopped fresh ginger
1½   tablespoons butter

Finely chop all peppercorns in processor. Rub pepper mixture over both sides of each steak. *(Can be prepared up to 4 hours ahead. Cover steaks with plastic wrap and refrigerate.)*

Heat oil in heavy medium skillet over high heat. Season steaks with salt. Add to skillet and cook to desired doneness, about 2 minutes per side for medium-rare. Transfer steaks to plate; tent with foil. Add Port, shallots and ginger to same skillet; boil until liquid is reduced to thin syrup, stirring frequently, about 5 minutes. Strain sauce into bowl, pressing on solids with spoon. Return sauce to same skillet; boil until thick syrup forms, about 2 minutes. Whisk in butter; season with salt. Spoon sauce around steaks and serve.

# THAI-STYLE BEEF AND RICE-NOODLE SALAD

## 2 SERVINGS; CAN BE DOUBLED

Purchased dumplings, such as wonton or *shao mai,* are a fine beginning for this meal (look for them in the freezer section of the supermarket); use hot mustard and soy sauce for dipping. To finish: a strawberry, banana and kiwi fruit salad sprinkled with coconut. (Pictured at right.)

5  tablespoons peanut oil
3  tablespoons rice vinegar
2  tablespoons minced peeled fresh ginger
2  large garlic cloves, chopped
1  tablespoon soy sauce
2  teaspoons hot chili sesame oil*

4  ounces snow peas, trimmed, cut in half diagonally if large
4  ounces dried Asian rice noodles,* broken in half

4  ounces purchased thinly sliced roast beef, cut crosswise into strips
¼  cup minced fresh cilantro
¼  cup chopped dry-roasted peanuts

Whisk first 6 ingredients together for dressing. Season to taste with salt and pepper. *(Can be prepared 1 day ahead. Cover dressing with plastic wrap and let stand at room temperature.)*

Cook peas in medium pot of boiling salted water until bright green, about 30 seconds. Using slotted spoon, transfer to colander and drain. Add noodles to same pot of boiling water and cook just until softened, about 2 minutes. Drain and rinse under cold water; drain well. Mix noodles and 6 tablespoons dressing in bowl. *(Snow peas and noodles can be made 2 hours ahead. Cover and let stand at room temperature.)*

Divide noodles between plates. Mix beef, cilantro, peanuts, snow peas and remaining dressing in medium bowl. Arrange beef mixture over noodles. Serve immediately.

*Available in the Asian foods section of most supermarkets.*

# STEAKS IN SHERRIED MUSHROOM SAUCE

## 2 SERVINGS; CAN BE DOUBLED

Sirloin or rib eye steaks also work well in this easy but sophisticated recipe. Team them with scalloped potatoes and green beans; finish with a fruit tart.

2  1-inch-thick beef tenderloin steaks  (each about 5 ounces)
1  tablespoon butter
3  tablespoons minced shallots
6  ounces mushrooms, thinly sliced
3  tablespoons dry Sherry
1  tablespoon chopped fresh parsley

Season steaks with salt and pepper. Melt butter in medium non-stick skillet over medium-high heat. Add steaks to skillet; cook to desired doneness about 4 minutes per side for medium-rare. Transfer to plates. Add shallots and mushrooms to skillet; sauté until mushrooms soften, about 5 minutes. Add Sherry; boil until liquid is reduced slightly and coats mushrooms, about 2 minutes. Spoon sauce over steaks. Garnish with parsley. Serve immediately.

# SESAME STEAK SALAD

4 SERVINGS; CAN BE DOUBLED

In keeping with the Asian-mixed-with-American theme here, fry up some frozen onion rings and dip them in hoisin sauce (available in the Asian section of most supermarkets). Shredded coconut sprinkled over vanilla ice cream would make a refreshing ending.

⅓ cup soy sauce
¼ cup rice wine vinegar
2 tablespoons vegetable oil
1 tablespoon oriental sesame oil
2 garlic cloves, minced
2 teaspoons finely grated peeled fresh ginger
1 teaspoon chili oil*

8 asparagus stalks, trimmed, cut into 1-inch pieces
8 large broccoli florets

12 ounces thinly sliced rare roast beef, cut into 3 x 1-inch strips
½ head savoy cabbage, shredded
½ large green bell pepper, thinly sliced
2 green onions, chopped

Whisk first 7 ingredients in medium bowl. Set aside.

Cook asparagus in large saucepan of boiling salted water until just crisp-tender. Drain. Refresh under cold water. Drain well. Repeat cooking process with broccoli florets.

Place beef in large bowl. Add dressing and marinate 5 minutes. Line platter with cabbage. Place asparagus and broccoli in center. Using tongs, remove beef from dressing. Arrange beef and bell pepper around edge of platter. Pour dressing over salad. Garnish with onions.

*Available in Asian markets and in many supermarkets.*

# SHORTCUT CORNED BEEF HASH

2 SERVINGS; CAN BE DOUBLED

Using frozen hash brown potatoes really reduces prep time here. This simple hash goes wonderfully with fried or poached eggs and steamed broccoli; finish with wedges of apple pie from your local bakery.

2½ cups frozen cubed hash brown potatoes, thawed
6 ounces diced cooked corned beef (about 1½ cups)
½ medium onion, chopped
½ medium green bell pepper, chopped
1 teaspoon dried thyme, crumbled
¼ teaspoon ground pepper
1½ tablespoons olive oil

Combine potatoes, corned beef, onion, bell pepper, thyme and pepper in medium bowl and toss to blend well. Heat oil in heavy medium skillet over medium heat. Add potato mixture and press to flatten with spatula. Cover and cook until bottom begins to crisp and brown, about 5 minutes. Using metal spatula, turn over browned bottom in sections. Cook uncovered until hash is thoroughly flecked with browned bits and onion and bell pepper are tender, turning over browned bottom in sections 2 more times, about 10 minutes longer.

## FILET MIGNONS WITH RED PEPPER SAUCE

2 SERVINGS; CAN BE DOUBLED

Topped with the brilliantly colored sauce and accompanied by herb-roasted potatoes and a watercress salad, this steak makes a very pretty plate. A purchased strawberry tart would be an equally elegant dessert.
(Pictured above.)

| 1 | 7½-ounce jar roasted red peppers, drained |
| 3 | tablespoons chopped shallots |
| 1 | tablespoon olive oil |
| 2 | teaspoons balsamic vinegar or red wine vinegar |
| 2 | ¾-inch-thick filet mignon steaks (about 6 ounces each) |

Puree roasted red peppers and chopped shallots in food processor. With machine running, gradually add olive oil and balsamic vinegar through food tube. Process until sauce is smooth. Season sauce to taste with salt and pepper. *(Can be prepared 1 day ahead. Cover and refrigerate. Bring to room temperature and stir before serving.)*

Prepare barbecue (medium-high heat) or preheat broiler. Season steaks lightly with salt and generous amount of pepper. Grill to desired doneness, about 4 minutes per side for medium-rare. Transfer steaks to plates. Spoon sauce over steaks and serve.

# TEXAS BEEF TACOS

6 SERVINGS; CAN BE DOUBLED

Stick to the southwestern theme by offering cups of black bean soup (spice it up with chopped fresh jalapeño chilies, if you like) and corn muffins before the tacos and pecan pie afterwards. (Pictured at left.)

| 1 | tablespoon corn oil |
| ½ | cup chopped onion |
| ½ | cup chopped green bell pepper |
| 3 | garlic cloves, chopped |
| 1 | tablespoon plus 1 teaspoon ground cumin |
| 1 | pound lean ground beef |
| ½ | cup tomato sauce |
| ¼ | cup raisins |
| ¼ | cup pecan pieces |
| ¼ | cup chopped fresh cilantro |
| 12 | taco shells or soft 6-inch-diameter corn tortillas |
| | Shredded lettuce |
| | Grated cheddar cheese |
| | Chopped fresh tomatoes |
| | Purchased salsa |

Heat oil in heavy large skillet over medium-high heat. Add onion, bell pepper and garlic and sauté until soft, about 5 minutes. Add cumin and stir 1 minute. Add ground beef and cook until brown, breaking up beef with back of fork, about 10 minutes. Spoon off any fat from pan. Add tomato sauce, raisins and pecans and cook until heated through, stirring occasionally, about 5 minutes. Mix in chopped cilantro. Season filling to taste with salt and pepper.

Spoon ¼ cup filling into each taco shell or spoon ¼ cup filling onto each tortilla and roll up. Serve, passing lettuce, cheese, tomatoes and salsa separately as garnishes.

# STEAK SANDWICHES WITH SAUTÉED MUSHROOMS

2 SERVINGS; CAN BE DOUBLED

Toss mixed greens with cherry tomatoes and blue cheese dressing to go with these sandwiches. For the finale: tropical fruit with coconut macaroons.

| 2 | tablespoons olive oil |
| 2 | 5- to 6-ounce cube steaks |
| 1½ | cups thinly sliced mushrooms (about 4 ounces) |
| 1 | teaspoon dried savory, crumbled |
| 4 | green onions, sliced |
| ½ | cup canned beef broth |
| 2 | thick slices country-style bread, toasted |

Heat 1 tablespoon oil in heavy medium skillet over high heat. Season steaks with salt and pepper. Add to skillet and sear 1 minute per side. Transfer to plate. Reduce heat to medium. Add remaining 1 tablespoon oil to same skillet. Add mushrooms and savory and sauté until mushrooms are brown, about 4 minutes. Add green onions and sauté 1 minute. Add broth and simmer until liquid thickens slightly, about 8 minutes. Return steaks and any juices to skillet. Reduce heat to medium-low. Cover and simmer until steaks are cooked through, 5 minutes. Arrange toast on plates. Top with steaks. Spoon sauce over.

# SPICY SESAME BEEF STIR-FRY

2 SERVINGS; CAN BE DOUBLED

After an appetizer of purchased egg rolls with hot mustard dip, serve steamed white rice alongside the beef. Sliced fresh oranges (mandarin or otherwise) and bananas sprinkled with chopped crystallized ginger complete the meal. (Pictured below.)

½    pound tender boneless beef (such as sirloin), cut crosswise into ¼-inch-thick slices
1½    tablespoons sesame seeds
1    large broccoli stalk
½    yellow bell pepper, thinly sliced
½    cup canned beef broth
2    tablespoons soy sauce
1    tablespoon minced peeled fresh ginger
1    large garlic clove, minced
1    teaspoon cornstarch
¼    teaspoon dried crushed red pepper

3    tablespoons vegetable oil
   Toasted sesame seeds (optional)

Combine beef strips with 1½ tablespoons sesame seeds in small bowl. Toss to coat well. Cut florets off broccoli stalk. Peel stalk and thinly slice crosswise. Combine broccoli florets and stalk with yellow pepper in medium bowl. Stir broth, soy sauce, ginger, garlic, cornstarch and crushed red pepper in small bowl until cornstarch dissolves.

Heat 1½ tablespoons oil in wok or heavy large skillet over high heat. Add beef and stir-fry until brown, about 2 minutes. Using slotted spoon, transfer beef to plate. Heat remaining 1½ tablespoons oil in wok. Add broccoli and peppers and cover wok. Cook until vegetables are just

tender, stirring occasionally, about 2 minutes. Stir broth mixture and add to wok. Add beef and any accumulated juices from plate. Simmer until sauce thickens, stirring occasionally, about 1 minute. Transfer beef mixture to platter. Sprinkle with toasted sesame seeds if desired.

❧

## MARINATED STEAK AND SUMMER SQUASH SALAD

2 SERVINGS; CAN BE DOUBLED

Serve this stylish salad with baked frozen french fries and slices of bread that have been topped with Parmesan and broiled. Finish with a lemon tart or lemon meringue pie from the bakery.

¼ cup olive oil
2½ tablespoons fresh lemon juice
1 garlic clove, minced
8 ounces thin flank steak or skirt steak
1 summer squash, cut lengthwise into ¼-inch-thick slices

4 cups bite-size pieces fresh spinach leaves
1 medium tomato, cut into wedges

Whisk oil, lemon juice and garlic in small bowl. Season with salt and pepper. Place steak and squash in shallow pan. Pour half of vinaigrette over. Turn steak and squash to coat. Let stand 20 minutes.

Prepare barbecue (medium-high heat). Season steak and squash with salt and pepper. Grill steak and squash until steak is medium-rare and squash is tender, about 3 minutes per side. Remove squash from grill. Transfer steak to cutting board and thinly slice across grain.

Divide spinach between 2 plates. Place tomato wedges on 1 side of plate. Place steak in center of plate. Drizzle with any accumulated juices. Place squash on side of plate opposite tomato wedges. Drizzle squash and tomato with remaining vinaigrette and serve.

❧

## STEAKS WITH BRANDY AND BLUE CHEESE

2 SERVINGS; CAN BE DOUBLED

Less than 15 minutes to an elegant steak dish. Begin the meal with something equally elegant, maybe pâté and crackers, and offer roasted potato wedges and steamed asparagus alongside. After dinner, have truffles.

1 tablespoon butter
2 6-ounce filet mignon steaks
⅔ cup canned beef broth
¼ cup brandy
1 teaspoon chopped fresh rosemary or ½ teaspoon dried
½ cup crumbled blue cheese

Melt butter in heavy medium skillet over medium-high heat. Season steaks with salt and pepper. Add steaks to skillet and sauté until cooked to desired doneness, about 4 minutes per side for medium-rare. Transfer steaks to plate. Add broth, brandy and rosemary to skillet and boil until sauce is reduced to ⅓ cup, scraping up browned bits, approximately 5 minutes. Spoon sauce over. Top each steak with half of blue cheese. Serve immediately.

# PEPPERED STEAK WITH MUSHROOMS

4 SERVINGS; CAN BE DOUBLED

When wild mushrooms are available, they can be mixed with the button mushrooms to turn this dish into a real treat. Broiled herbed tomatoes and new potatoes with parsley would be delicious served alongside the main course. Raspberry sorbet is an instant and refreshing finale.

| 4 | 1-inch-thick filet mignon steaks (about 5 ounces each) |
| 2 | teaspoons cracked black peppercorns |
| 2½ | tablespoons unsalted butter |
| 1 | tablespoon vegetable oil |
| ¼ | cup minced shallots (about 1 large) |
| 1 | pound mushrooms, thickly sliced |
| ½ | teaspoon dried tarragon, crumbled |
| ⅓ | cup dry white wine |
| 2 | tablespoons Cognac or brandy |

Season steaks with salt. Pat pepper firmly onto both sides. Melt 1 tablespoon butter with oil in heavy large skillet over high heat. Sauté steaks until brown and cooked to desired doneness, about 4 minutes per side for medium-rare. Transfer steaks to platter.

Melt remaining 1½ tablespoons butter in same skillet over medium-high heat. Add shallots and stir to coat with butter. Add mushrooms and tarragon and cook until mushrooms are tender, stirring frequently, about 5 minutes. Add wine and Cognac to skillet and simmer 1 minute, scraping up browned bits from bottom of pan. Return steaks and any accumulated juices to skillet. Cook steaks until just heated through, about 2 minutes. Arrange steaks on plates. Spoon mushrooms around steaks; spoon pan juices over and serve.

# SLOPPY JOES

4 SERVINGS; CAN BE DOUBLED

We love to spoon this flavorful mixture over split, toasted kaiser rolls. Garnish the sandwiches with crisp shredded lettuce. To complete the menu, top lemon ice cream with blueberry sauce and lots of fresh blueberries.

| 1 | tablespoon olive oil |
| 1½ | pounds ground beef |
| 2 | medium onions, chopped |
| 1 | green bell pepper, chopped |
| 4 | large garlic cloves, chopped |
| 1½ | tablespoons chili powder |
| 2 | 28-ounce cans Italian plum tomatoes, drained, chopped |
| ½ | cup bottled chili sauce |
| ½ | cup canned beef broth |
| 2 | teaspoons red wine vinegar |
| 1½ | teaspoons Worcestershire sauce |
| 3 | tablespoons chopped fresh parsley |

Heat olive oil in heavy large skillet over high heat. Add beef and cook until beginning to lose pink color, breaking up with fork, about 5 minutes. Reduce heat to medium. Mix in onions, green bell pepper and garlic. Cook until vegetables begin to soften, stirring occasionally, about 5 minutes. Mix in chili powder and stir 1 minute. Add tomatoes, chili sauce, broth, vinegar and Worcestershire sauce. Cook until vegetables are tender and mixture is thick, stirring occasionally, about 15 minutes. Season to taste with salt and pepper. *(Can be prepared 1 day ahead. Cover and refrigerate. Rewarm over low heat before continuing.)* Mix in parsley.

# Sautéed Calf's Liver with Raisins and Onions

2 SERVINGS; CAN BE DOUBLED

Roasted red potatoes and steamed green beans are good accompaniments. Papaya halves with a squeeze of fresh lime would be a refreshing dessert. (Pictured below.)

| | |
|---|---|
| 2 | tablespoons raisins |
| | Warm water |
| 1½ | tablespoons olive oil |
| 8 | ounces calf's liver (about 4 thin slices) |
| 1 | large onion, thinly sliced |
| 2 | tablespoons balsamic vinegar or red wine vinegar |

Place raisins in small bowl. Cover with warm water. Let stand 10 minutes to plump; drain raisins well.

Heat olive oil in heavy medium skillet over medium-high heat. Season liver with salt and pepper. Sauté until brown but still rare, about 1 minute per side. Transfer liver to plate. Add sliced onion to same skillet. Sauté until onion is brown and soft, about 10 minutes. Add balsamic vinegar and raisins and stir 30 seconds, scraping up browned bits. Return liver and any accumulated juices to pan. Cook until liver is heated through, approximately 2 minutes.

Arrange liver on plates. Spoon onion mixture over and serve.

## Veal Scallops with Cranberry-Citrus Compote

2 SERVINGS; CAN BE DOUBLED

If dried cranberries are not available, chopped dried apricots can be substituted. Herbed rice pilaf and steamed broccoli make nice accompaniments, with a purchased chocolate cake for dessert. (Pictured at right.)

⅓ cup dried cranberries (about 1 ounce)
3 tablespoons boiling water
3 tablespoons orange juice
1 tablespoon bourbon
1 teaspoon minced orange peel
½ teaspoon minced peeled fresh ginger or ¼ teaspoon ground

1½ tablespoons unsalted butter
8 ounces thin veal scallops
1 green onion, minced

Combine dried cranberries and boiling water in small bowl. Let stand 10 minutes. Add orange juice, bourbon, orange peel and ginger; stir to blend. *(Can be made 3 hours ahead. Cover cranberry mixture and let stand at room temperature.)*

Melt butter in heavy large skillet over medium-high heat. Season veal with salt and pepper. Add veal to skillet and sauté until brown and just cooked through, about 2 minutes per side. Using tongs, transfer veal to plates. Add cranberry mixture to skillet and cook until mixture thickens, scraping up any browned bits, about 1 minute. Mix in green onion. Season compote with salt and pepper. Spoon over veal.

## Veal Chops Provençale

4 SERVINGS; CAN BE DOUBLED

Serve buttered orzo (rice-shaped pasta) and steamed zucchini rounds as accompaniments, then pass sugared orange slices and purchased almond cookies to finish.

3 tablespoons olive oil
4 1-inch-thick veal loin chops (about 2 pounds total)

1 green bell pepper, cut into strips
1 large garlic clove, chopped
1 1-pound can Italian plum tomatoes, chopped, juices reserved
½ cup dry white wine
6 large oil-packed sun-dried tomatoes, drained, chopped
1½ teaspoons dried oregano, crumbled
⅓ cup Niçoise olives

Heat oil in heavy large skillet over high heat. Season veal on both sides with pepper. Add veal to skillet and cook until brown and just cooked through, about 5 minutes per side for medium-rare. Transfer veal chops to plate. Set veal aside.

Add green pepper and garlic to same skillet. Sauté 1 minute. Add plum tomatoes and their juices, wine, sun-dried tomatoes and oregano. Bring mixture to boil, scraping up browned bits. Cook until mixture thickens, stirring occasionally, about 10 minutes. Return veal and any accumulated juices to skillet. Add olives and cook until veal is just heated through. Season with salt and pepper. Arrange veal chops on platter. Spoon sauce over and serve.

# VEAL CHOPS WITH TOMATO RELISH

**4 SERVINGS; CAN BE DOUBLED**

Sun-dried tomatoes combine with fresh plum tomatoes in this relish. Serve with buttered fettuccine noodles, steamed yellow or green beans, and apricot halves drizzled with Amaretto for an elegant *and* easy dessert. (Pictured below.)

| | |
|---|---|
| ¼ | cup finely chopped drained oil-packed sun-dried tomatoes |
| ½ | pound finely chopped plum tomatoes |
| 1 | garlic clove, minced |
| 2 | tablespoons minced fresh basil or ½ teaspoon dried, crumbled and mixed with 2 tablespoons minced fresh parsley |
| 1½ | tablespoons olive oil |
| 1 | teaspoon balsamic vinegar or red wine vinegar |
| ¼ to ½ | Hot pepper sauce (such as Tabasco) |
| 4 | 1-inch-thick loin, rib or T-bone veal chops (about 8 ounces each) |
| 2 | tablespoons olive oil |

In medium bowl, combine sun-dried tomatoes, plum tomatoes, garlic, basil, 1½ tablespoons olive oil, balsamic vinegar and hot sauce to taste. Cover and let stand at room temperature at least 15 minutes. *(Tomato relish can be prepared 4 hours ahead.)*

Prepare barbecue (high heat). Season both sides of veal chops lightly with salt and pepper. Brush both sides with olive oil. Cook chops to desired doneness, about 5 minutes per side for medium-rare. Transfer cooked chops to platter. Spoon ¼ of tomato relish atop each chop.

# VEAL SALTIMBOCCA

2 SERVINGS; CAN BE DOUBLED

Steamed broccoli and buttered orzo (rice-shaped pasta) make fine accompaniments to the veal, with an almond tart and espresso to finish.

| | |
|---|---|
| 8 | ounces veal scaloppine (about 4 pieces) |
| ½ | teaspoon dried rubbed sage |
| 1½ | tablespoons butter |
| 2 | large thin prosciutto slices, halved (about 1 ounce) |
| 4 | thin slices Italian Fontina cheese (about 1½ ounces) |
| ¼ | cup dry Marsala |

Sprinkle both sides of veal with sage; season with pepper. Melt butter in heavy large skillet over medium-high heat. Add veal and sauté until brown on first side, about 1 minute. Turn veal over. Layer 1 prosciutto piece and 1 cheese slice on cooked side of each veal piece. Cover pan, reduce heat and cook just until cheese melts, about 1 minute. Using spatula, transfer veal to platter. Add Marsala to skillet. Increase heat to medium-high and cook until sauce is slightly reduced, scraping up any browned bits, about 1 minute. Season to taste with salt and pepper. Spoon sauce over veal and then serve.

# VEAL CHOPS WITH DOUBLE-MUSTARD SAUCE

4 SERVINGS; CAN BE DOUBLED

Fill tomato halves with sautéed spinach, sprinkle with freshly grated Parmesan cheese and bake until cooked through for a fast and unusual side dish. After dinner, slices of Linzertorte with cups of coffee would be just the thing.

| | |
|---|---|
| 8 | tablespoons (1 stick) butter, room temperature |
| 3 | tablespoons minced shallots |
| 2 | tablespoons Dijon mustard |
| 1½ | tablespoons chopped fresh tarragon |
| 1 | tablespoon coarse-grained French mustard |
| 4 | veal chops (about ½ to ¾ inch thick) |
| 2 | teaspoons Dijon mustard |
| 4 | teaspoons whole mustard seeds |
| ⅔ | cup dry vermouth |

Combine 7 tablespoons butter with next 4 ingredients in bowl. Season with pepper. *(Can be made 4 days ahead. Cover and chill.)*

Brush veal with 2 teaspoons Dijon mustard. Press 1 teaspoon mustard seeds onto 1 side of each veal chop. Season with salt and pepper. Melt remaining 1 tablespoon butter in heavy large skillet over medium heat. Add veal and cook until just cooked through, about 4 minutes per side. Transfer to plate; cover with foil and keep warm. Add vermouth to drippings in skillet; boil until liquid is reduced to ¼ cup, about 3 minutes. Whisk in mustard butter. Season to taste with salt and pepper. Drizzle sauce over veal and serve.

# VEAL CHOPS WITH TARRAGON

2 SERVINGS; CAN BE DOUBLED

Serve the chops on a bed of mashed potatoes to catch the flavorful juices, along with buttered baby squashes for color. Splurge on Napoleon pastries from a nearby bakery for dessert.

2   ½-inch-thick veal loin chops (7 to 8 ounces each)
2   teaspoons dried tarragon, crumbled
    All purpose flour
2   tablespoons unsalted butter
½   cup dry white wine
½   cup canned chicken broth
2   tablespoons fresh lemon juice

Season veal with salt, pepper and 1 teaspoon tarragon; dust lightly with flour. Melt butter in heavy medium skillet over medium-high heat. Add veal and cook until light brown and just cooked through, about 4 minutes per side. Transfer veal to plate. Add wine, broth, lemon juice and remaining 1 teaspoon tarragon to skillet. Boil until juices are syrupy, scraping up any browned bits, about 5 minutes. Return veal and any collected juices to skillet and cook until just heated through, about 1 minute. Serve immediately.

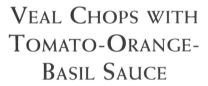

# VEAL CHOPS WITH TOMATO-ORANGE-BASIL SAUCE

4 SERVINGS; CAN BE DOUBLED

This delicious sauce is also very nice with chicken and shellfish. Serve the chops with a spinach salad and buttered noodles. A dense bakery chocolate cake completes this elegant meal.

¾   cup orange juice
½   cup dry white wine
¼   cup minced shallots
2   tablespoons minced orange peel (orange part only)
¼   cup whipping cream

5   tablespoons butter
4   6-ounce veal loin chops

1   cup chopped seeded tomato
¼   cup thinly sliced fresh basil or 1½ teaspoons dried, crumbled
    Fresh basil sprigs (optional)

Combine first 3 ingredients and 1 tablespoon orange peel in heavy small saucepan. Boil until mixture is reduced to 3 tablespoons, about 10 minutes. Add cream and boil 1 minute. Set sauce aside. *(Can be prepared 1 day ahead. Cover and refrigerate.)*

Melt 1 tablespoon butter in heavy large skillet over medium heat. Season veal with salt and pepper. Sauté veal until just cooked through, about 4 minutes per side. Transfer to plates; keep warm.

Reheat sauce over low heat. Whisk in remaining 4 tablespoons butter. Stir in tomato, sliced basil and remaining 1 tablespoon orange peel. Season to taste with salt and pepper. Ladle sauce over veal. Garnish with basil sprigs if desired.

# Swedish Meatballs with Dill Sauce

2 SERVINGS; CAN BE DOUBLED

Braised red cabbage and buttered noodles make fine accompaniments for these delicate meatballs. A spice layer cake and mugs of hot cinnamon tea top off the comforting meal. (Pictured below.)

| 8 | ounces ground veal |
| ⅓ | cup fresh white breadcrumbs |
| ⅓ | cup minced onion |
| 1 | egg white |
| 2 | tablespoons minced fresh dill or 2 teaspoons dillweed |

| 2 | teaspoons vegetable oil |
| ⅓ | cup half and half |
| ¼ | cup whipping cream |

Line small baking pan with waxed paper. Combine veal, breadcrumbs, onion, egg white and 1½ tablespoons dill in large bowl and blend well. Shape veal mixture into about 16 balls and place on prepared pan. *(Can be prepared 1 day ahead. Cover and refrigerate.)*

Heat oil in medium nonstick skillet over medium heat. Add meatballs to skillet; cook until brown and cooked through, turning frequently, about 12 minutes. Add half and half, whipping cream and ½ tablespoon dill to skillet; stir until sauce is slightly thickened, scraping up any browned bits, about 3 minutes. Season with salt and pepper.

# LAMB CHOPS ON WARM LENTIL SALAD

2 SERVINGS; CAN BE DOUBLED

Oysters on the half shell sprinkled with fresh lemon juice would make a festive start to this meal, with broccoli and crusty bread to accompany the lamb, and fruit compote for dessert.

| | |
|---|---|
| 1½ | cups water |
| ½ | cup lentils, picked over, rinsed, drained |
| 2 | teaspoons dried mint, crumbled |
| 2½ | tablespoons olive oil |
| 2 | 1½-inch-thick loin lamb chops, well trimmed (about 6 ounces each) |
| 1 | small red bell pepper, diced |
| 2 | green onions, sliced |
| 1 | tablespoon balsamic vinegar or red wine vinegar |

Bring water to boil in heavy small saucepan. Add lentils and mint; season with salt and pepper. Cover pan, reduce heat to low and simmer until lentils are tender, about 30 minutes. Drain any excess cooking liquid from lentils if necessary.

Meanwhile, heat ½ tablespoon olive oil in heavy medium skillet over medium-high heat. Season lamb chops with salt and pepper. Sauté lamb chops until brown on outside but still pink inside, about 7 minutes per side. Transfer lamb to plate. Add remaining 2 tablespoons oil, diced red bell pepper and sliced green onions to same skillet. Stir until vegetables just begin to soften, about 2 minutes. Add balsamic vinegar to skillet and scrape up any browned bits.

Add lentils to vegetables and toss to coat well with dressing. Season lentils with salt and pepper. Divide lentil salad between plates. Arrange lamb chops on lentils and serve.

# LAMB WITH WHITE BEANS AND TOMATOES

2 SERVINGS; CAN BE DOUBLED

The classic version of this dish is prepared with a roasted leg of lamb and a long-simmered sauce of white beans and tomatoes. Our adaptation is excellent with a loaf of crusty bread, some lettuce leaves tossed with a mustard vinaigrette, and a glass of dry red wine. Fresh fruit and butter cookies are a nice combination for dessert.

| | |
|---|---|
| 1 | pound boneless loin lamb chops, trimmed, cut into 1½-inch cubes |
| 1 | tablespoon unsalted butter |
| 1½ | teaspoons chopped garlic |
| ½ | cup dry white wine |
| 1 | teaspoon dried rosemary, crumbled |
| 1 | cup drained canned cannellini (white kidney beans) or other white beans |
| 1 | 14½-ounce can stewed tomatoes |

Season lamb with salt and pepper on all sides. Melt butter in heavy large skillet over medium-high heat. Add lamb and cook until brown on all sides, stirring frequently, about 3 minutes. Add garlic and stir 30 seconds. Add wine and rosemary. Increase heat to high and cook 30 seconds, scraping up any browned bits. Stir in cannellini and tomatoes with their juices, breaking up tomatoes with back of spoon. Reduce heat to medium-low. Simmer uncovered until lamb is cooked through and sauce thickens slightly, about 10 minutes.

## SPICED LAMB
## BURGERS

2 SERVINGS; CAN BE DOUBLED

Serve these big burgers in whole wheat pita bread. Garnish the sandwiches with sliced tomatoes, cucumbers, lettuce and a cool dollop of yogurt. Pour iced mint tea along with the meal, and buy some baklava and apricots for the finale. (Pictured above.)

¾   pound lean ground lamb
½   cup finely chopped onion
1   large garlic clove, minced
3   tablespoons chopped fresh mint or 1 teaspoon dried, crumbled
1   teaspoon ground cumin
½   teaspoon ground coriander

2   whole wheat pita bread rounds, top third cut off

Prepare barbecue (medium-high heat). Combine ground lamb, onion, garlic, mint, cumin and coriander in medium bowl. Season with salt and pepper. Shape lamb into two ¾-inch-thick rounds. Grill burgers to desired doneness, about 5 minutes per side for medium-rare.

Open pita breads and place 1 burger in each. Serve hot.

# Spring Lamb Stew

2 SERVINGS; CAN BE DOUBLED

Dinner rolls and a green salad with lemon vinaigrette would go well with this quick-cooking stew. Strawberries and cream are a great finish. (Pictured at right.)

12 ounces lean boneless leg of lamb or trimmed boneless sirloin chops, cut into ½-inch pieces
2 tablespoons all purpose flour

2 tablespoons vegetable oil
2 large garlic cloves, chopped
1 teaspoon dried thyme, crumbled
12 ounces boiling potatoes, peeled, cut into 1-inch pieces
6 ounces peeled baby carrots
1 cup canned beef broth
1 cup frozen green peas, thawed

Place lamb pieces in mixing bowl. Season to taste with salt and pepper. Add flour and toss well to coat.

Heat oil in heavy large saucepan over high heat. Add lamb; cook until brown, stirring frequently, about 5 minutes. Reduce heat to medium-low. Add garlic and thyme and cook 30 seconds. Add potatoes, carrots and broth. Bring stew just to simmer. Cover and cook until lamb and vegetables are just tender, about 20 minutes. *(Can be made 1 day ahead. Cover and chill. Rewarm gently before continuing.)* Add peas to stew and simmer until heated through. Season with salt and pepper.

# Home-Style Shepherd's Pie

2 SERVINGS; CAN BE DOUBLED

Steamed petit peas are a fitting partner to this dish. Try ice cream topped with chopped fruits for dessert.

8 ounces ground lamb
1 medium onion, chopped
2 large garlic cloves, minced
1 14½-ounce can Italian-style stewed tomatoes
2 cups mashed potatoes, room temperature
2 tablespoons grated Parmesan cheese

Preheat oven to 500°F. Stir lamb, onion and garlic in heavy medium saucepan over medium heat until lamb is light brown and onion is tender, about 5 minutes. Increase heat to high. Mix in stewed tomatoes with their juices and cook until almost all liquid evaporates, breaking up tomatoes with back of spoon, about 10 minutes. Season with salt and pepper. Spoon mixture into 9-inch-diameter glass pie dish. Drop mashed potatoes by tablespoonfuls atop lamb mixture, covering completely. Sprinkle with cheese. Bake until potatoes are light golden, about 15 minutes. Serve immediately.

# LAMB WITH ROSEMARY BROTH AND VEGETABLES

4 SERVINGS; CAN BE DOUBLED

Offer hot English mustard with this one-pot meal, along with thick slices of country-style bread spread with whipped butter. Finish up with chocolate-dipped strawberries.

1¼ cups canned low-salt chicken broth
⅔ cup diced peeled carrot
½ cup diced peeled rutabaga
½ cup diced peeled turnip
⅔ cup diced unpeeled zucchini

4 ½-inch-thick boneless lamb sirloin chops (about 5 ounces each)
2 fresh rosemary sprigs or ½ teaspoon dried, crumbled
1¼ teaspoons cornstarch
1 tablespoon water
1 tablespoon capers

1 teaspoon unsalted butter
Pinch of ground nutmeg
2 tablespoons chopped chopped fresh chives or green onions

Bring broth to boil in large saucepan. Add next 3 ingredients and cook until crisp-tender, about 4 minutes. Using slotted spoon, transfer vegetables to plate. Add zucchini to broth; cook until crisp-tender, 2 minutes. Transfer to plate with vegetables, using slotted spoon.

Add lamb and rosemary to broth. Bring to boil; reduce heat and simmer until lamb chops are just pink inside, about 5 minutes. Transfer lamb to platter; cover with foil. Strain broth into small saucepan and bring to boil. Dissolve cornstarch in 1 tablespoon water. Add to broth and simmer until slightly thickened, stirring constantly, about 2 minutes. Stir in capers. Season with salt and pepper. Keep warm.

Melt butter in medium saucepan over medium-high heat. Add vegetables and nutmeg and sauté until heated through, about 3 minutes. Season to taste with salt and pepper. Stir in chives.

Divide vegetables among 4 plates. Cut each lamb chop crosswise into 3 pieces; arrange over vegetables. Pour sauce over lamb.

❧

# LAMB CHOPS WITH CHUTNEY CRUST

4 SERVINGS; CAN BE DOUBLED

Toss orzo, that rice-shaped pasta, with raisins, chopped fresh cilantro and butter for a simple pilaf to go with the chops, and for dessert, sandwich ladyfingers with lemon curd from a jar.

1 cup fresh breadcrumbs
¼ teaspoon dried rosemary, crumbled
4 2-inch-thick lamb loin chops
4 tablespoons Major Grey's chutney

Preheat oven to 450°F. Butter small baking sheet. Combine breadcrumbs and rosemary on plate. Season with salt and pepper. Season lamb chops generously with salt and pepper. Spread each side of chops with ½ tablespoon chutney. Dip each chop into breadcrumb mixture to coat. Transfer to prepared baking sheet. Bake until crumbs are golden brown and lamb is cooked to desired doneness, about 15 minutes for medium-rare. Transfer to plates and serve.

# ROAST RACK OF LAMB WITH PARSLEYED CRUMBS

2 SERVINGS; CAN BE DOUBLED

Coat very small red potatoes with olive oil and cook alongside the lamb, and steam some green beans to round out the main course. Pass a plate of bittersweet chocolate cookies with cups of cappuccino for dessert. (Pictured above.)

| 1 | well-trimmed 1½-pound rack of lamb, room temperature |
| 3 | tablespoons coarse-grained mustard |
| ½ | cup fresh breadcrumbs |
| ¼ | cup minced fresh parsley |
| 1 | teaspoon dried rosemary, crumbled |
| 1 | garlic clove, minced |

Position rack in center of oven and preheat oven to 450°F. Season lamb with salt and pepper. Brush lamb with 1 tablespoon mustard. In small bowl, combine remaining 2 tablespoons mustard with remaining ingredients. Press crumb mixture evenly over top of lamb.

Arrange lamb crumb side up in roasting pan. Roast 10 minutes. Reduce heat 400°F and roast until thermometer inserted into center of meaty part registers 135°F for medium-rare, about 15 minutes longer. Carve lamb, cutting between ribs, and serve.

# LAMB KEBABS WITH PEANUT SAUCE

2 SERVINGS; CAN BE DOUBLED

Stop by your local Indian take-out place for a starter to go with these delicious kebabs, which get served with rice. To finish up, sprinkle mint liqueur over fresh mango and papaya slices.
(Pictured at left.)

¾ cup canned chicken broth
½ cup milk
1 cup creamy peanut butter (do not use old-fashioned style or freshly ground)
2 teaspoons ground cumin
2 teaspoons curry powder
1 to 2 tablespoons fresh lime juice

14 ounces boneless leg of lamb, cut into 12 1½-inch cubes
1 medium onion, cut into 12 pieces
1 small red bell pepper, cut into 12 squares
4 12-inch-long wooden skewers, soaked in water 30 minutes
Freshly cooked rice

Bring broth and milk to simmer in heavy small saucepan over medium heat. Add peanut butter and stir until smooth and heated through. Mix in cumin, curry powder and lime juice to taste. Season with salt and pepper. Remove from heat.

Preheat broiler. Alternate 3 lamb cubes, 3 onion pieces and 3 bell pepper squares on each skewer. Season to taste with salt and pepper. Brush kebabs with peanut sauce. Broil kebabs to desired doneness, about 5 minutes per side for medium-rare. Serve lamb kebabs with rice, passing remaining peanut sauce separately.

# LAMB CHOPS WITH ROSEMARY-MINT SAUCE

2 SERVINGS; CAN BE DOUBLED

Rice pilaf and sautéed Swiss chard would be nice accompaniments, and sweetened strawberries spooned over toasted pound cake, a fitting dessert.

2 large garlic cloves, peeled
1 teaspoon salt
1 teaspoon ground pepper
2 teaspoons olive oil
4 4-ounce loin lamb chops

3 tablespoons mint jelly
3 tablespoons white wine vinegar
1 teaspoon minced fresh rosemary or ½ teaspoon dried, crumbled

Chop garlic with salt and pepper on cutting board, then use flat side of knife blade to mash garlic mixture to paste. Scrape paste into small bowl and mix in oil. Rub garlic paste on both sides of lamb chops. Let lamb chops stand for 10 minutes.

Meanwhile, stir mint jelly, vinegar and rosemary in small saucepan over high heat until jelly melts and mixture boils. Reduce heat to medium and cook until sauce reduces slightly to syrup, 2 minutes.

Preheat broiler. Broil lamb until well-browned but still pink inside, 4 minutes per side. Arrange chops on plates. Spoon sauce over.

# MEDALLIONS OF PORK WITH PEAR SAUCE

4 SERVINGS; CAN BE DOUBLED

Sautéed cabbage and potatoes would complete this satisfying main course. Wrap things up with individual servings of old-fashioned chocolate pudding. (Pictured above.)

2    tablespoons vegetable oil
4    ½-inch-thick boneless pork loin chops
     Dried rubbed sage
     All purpose flour

2    pears, peeled, cored, thinly sliced (about 1 pound)
⅓    cup dry white wine
2    tablespoons sugar
2    tablespoons chopped crystallized ginger

Heat oil in heavy large skillet over medium heat. Season pork with dried sage, salt and pepper. Coat pork with flour; shake off excess. Sauté pork until brown, about 3 minutes per side. Transfer to platter.

Drain fat from skillet. Add pears and sauté over medium heat 2 minutes. Stir in wine, sugar and ginger, scraping up any browned bits. Increase heat to high and boil until pears are tender and syrup is thick, about 5 minutes. Return pork and any accumulated juices to skillet. Simmer just until cooked through, about 1 minute. Season to taste with salt and pepper. Arrange pork on plates. Spoon sauce over and serve.

# MAPLE MUSTARD-GLAZED HAM STEAK

2 SERVINGS; CAN BE DOUBLED

Alongside the ham, serve parsley-topped steamed red potatoes and some watercress tossed with a shallot vinaigrette. Vanilla custard makes a light and creamy dessert.

| | |
|---|---|
| 1 | 8-ounce ham steak |
| 1 | tablespoon butter |
| 2 | tablespoons pure maple syrup |
| 2 | to 3 teaspoons Dijon mustard |
| 2 | teaspoons cider vinegar |

Cut ham into 2 pieces. Season generously with pepper. Melt butter in heavy medium skillet over medium-high heat. Add ham and cook until golden brown, about 3 minutes per side. Transfer ham to platter. Whisk maple syrup, mustard and vinegar into drippings in skillet. Cook until smooth glaze forms, whisking frequently, about 1 minute. Spoon glaze over ham and serve.

# PORK BRAISED WITH AROMATIC VEGETABLES

2 SERVINGS; CAN BE DOUBLED

Start with a salad of red leaf lettuce and curly endive tossed with balsamic vinegar and extra-virgin olive oil. Accompany the pork with buttered egg noodles garnished with parsley and roasted red pepper strips. As a finale: a purchased fresh pear tart.

| | |
|---|---|
| 1 | 8- to 10-ounce pork tenderloin |
| 2 | tablespoons olive oil |
| 1 | carrot, thinly sliced |
| 1 | small celery stalk, thinly sliced |
| 1 | medium parsnip, thinly sliced |
| 2 | large garlic cloves, minced |
| ⅔ | cup canned low-salt chicken broth |
| ½ | teaspoon dried thyme, crumbled |
| 1 | tablespoon Dijon mustard |

Cut pork in half crosswise. Season with salt and pepper. Heat 1 tablespoon oil in heavy medium skillet over medium-high heat. Add pork and cook until brown on all sides, about 6 minutes. Using tongs, transfer pork to plate. Set aside.

Reduce heat to medium-low. Add remaining 1 tablespoon oil to skillet. Add carrot, celery, parsnip and garlic. Cook 2 minutes, stirring occasionally. Add broth and thyme. Return pork and any juices on plate to skillet. Bring liquids to simmer. Cover skillet and simmer until pork is cooked through, about 10 minutes. Remove pork. Add mustard to skillet. Increase heat to high and cook until sauce thickens, whisking occasionally, about 5 minutes. Slice pork crosswise on diagonal. Fan slices on plates. Spoon sauce and vegetables alongside pork and serve.

# Bourbon-barbecued Ribs

2 SERVINGS; CAN BE DOUBLED

This sauce would also taste good with pork chops. Team the main course with coleslaw and french fries (the frozen kind are perfectly acceptable here). Serve watermelon wedges and giant chocolate chip cookies for a nice ending.

1 tablespoon vegetable oil
1 medium onion, thinly sliced
1 teaspoon dried thyme, crumbled
3 tablespoons bourbon
½ cup purchased barbecue sauce

1 baby back rib rack, cut into two 5- or 6-rib pieces

Heat oil in heavy medium saucepan over medium-high heat. Add onion and sauté until beginning to soften, about 5 minutes. Add thyme and sauté 1 minute. Add bourbon and simmer until mixture is reduced to glaze, about 1 minute. Mix in barbecue sauce. *(Can be prepared 1 day ahead. Cover and refrigerate.)*

Prepare barbecue (medium-high heat). Season ribs with salt and pepper; grill 5 minutes per side. Brush with sauce; continue grilling until cooked through, brushing with sauce and turning every 5 minutes, about 15 minutes longer. Arrange ribs on plates. Spoon remaining sauce alongside. Serve immediately.

# Grilled Pork Saté

2 SERVINGS; CAN BE DOUBLED

A favorite treat that it sold by street vendors from Thailand to Indonesia, *saté* is made by pairing grilled skewered meats with a spicy peanut sauce. Serve atop a shredded lettuce and radish salad with sesame vinaigrette and accompany with pita bread. To conclude, pass a plate of ginger cookies and a bowl of melon balls drizzled with honey.

3 tablespoons chunky peanut butter
2 tablespoons fresh lime juice
2 tablespoons low-sodium soy sauce
1 tablespoon minced peeled fresh ginger
2 small garlic cloves, minced
¼ teaspoon (generous) dried crushed red pepper
8 to 10 ounces pork cutlets (about ¼ inch thick), cut into ½-inch-wide strips
4 8-inch bamboo skewers, soaked in water 10 minutes

¼ cup thinly sliced green onions

Prepare barbecue (medium-high heat). Whisk peanut butter, lime juice, soy sauce, ginger, garlic and crushed red pepper in shallow baking dish until combined. Set aside 2 tablespoons sauce. Add pork strips to remaining sauce in baking dish and toss to coat completely. Thread pork strips onto skewers. Let stand 10 minutes.

Grill until pork is slightly charred and cooked through, about 3 minutes per side. Brush with reserved 2 tablespoons sauce and cook 30 seconds. Transfer to platter. Sprinkle with green onions and serve.

# PORK CUTLETS WITH MUSTARD-MAPLE SAUCE

2 SERVINGS; CAN BE DOUBLED

This savory-sweet sauce goes beautifully with steamed asparagus and rice tossed with chopped raw tomato and sliced green onions. To finish, offer slices of bakery chocolate cake.
(Pictured below.)

| | |
|---|---|
| 4 | boneless pork loin chops (cutlets) |
| 3 | teaspoons minced fresh sage or 1 teaspoon dried, crumbled |
| 1 | tablespoon butter |
| ½ | cup canned low-salt chicken broth |
| 1 | tablespoon pure maple syrup |
| 1 | tablespoon coarse-grained mustard |

Place boneless pork chops between sheets of plastic wrap and pound to thickness of ⅓ inch. Sprinkle pork chops with 1½ teaspoons sage, salt and generous amount of pepper. Set aside.

Melt butter in heavy medium skillet over medium-high heat. Add pork and cook until brown on both sides and cooked through, about 1½ minutes per side. Transfer pork to plate, leaving drippings in skillet. Add broth, maple syrup, mustard and remaining 1½ teaspoons sage to skillet. Boil until syrupy, scraping up browned bits, about 3 minutes. Reduce heat to low. Return pork and any accumulated juices to skillet and cook until just heated through, about 1 minute. Serve.

# Pork Chops Braised with Cider and Apples

4 SERVINGS; CAN BE DOUBLED

Serve side dishes of steamed green beans and buttered noodles sprinkled with poppy seeds. Then offer herb teas with a plate of purchased peanut butter cookies and sugar cookies. (Pictured at right.)

4 ¾-inch-thick center-cut pork chops
1 tablespoon vegetable oil

2 tablespoons (¼ stick) butter
1 large onion, thinly sliced
1 small tart apple, cored, thinly sliced
½ cup apple cider
1½ tablespoons apple cider vinegar
1 bay leaf

Season pork chops generously with salt and pepper. Heat oil in heavy large skillet over medium-high heat. Add pork to skillet and cook until brown and cooked through, about 5 minutes per side. Transfer pork to platter. Tent with foil to keep warm.

Drain off all but 1 tablespoon drippings from skillet. Add butter to skillet and melt over medium heat. Add onion and apple to skillet and sauté until onion is almost soft, about 5 minutes. Mix in cider, vinegar and bay leaf. Cover skillet and cook until onions and apples are tender, about 10 minutes. Discard bay leaf. Add any accumulated juices from pork chop platter to skillet. Increase heat and cook until sauce thickens slightly, 3 minutes. Spoon sauce over pork and serve.

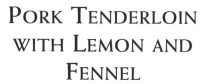

# Pork Tenderloin with Lemon and Fennel

4 SERVINGS; CAN BE DOUBLED

Serve spaghetti squash tossed with butter and chopped tomatoes alongside the herb-marinated tenderloins; crisp breadsticks are another nice touch. Finish with a purchased plum pie.

2 teaspoons fennel seeds
¼ cup olive oil
4 large garlic cloves, minced
2 teaspoons grated lemon peel
1 teaspoon salt
1 teaspoon pepper
2 pork tenderloins (about ¾ pound each)

Lemon slices

Crush fennel seeds in spice grinder or in mortar with pestle. Combine fennel seeds with oil, garlic, lemon peel, salt and pepper in small bowl. Spread half of mixture over tenderloins; reserve remainder for serving. *(Can be prepared 8 hours ahead. Cover tenderloins and reserved seasoning separately and chill.)*

Preheat oven to 500°F. Place tenderloins on rack in baking pan. Place pan in oven and reduce temperature to 475°F. Roast pork until thermometer inserted into center registers 150°F, about 22 minutes. Let stand 5 minutes. Slice thinly on diagonal. Arrange slices on platter. Spoon reserved seasoning mixture over. Garnish with lemon slices.

# SAUSAGES AND WHITE BEANS ON ARUGULA

2 SERVINGS; CAN BE DOUBLED

Complete this one-pot meal with some bread and an easy dessert—maybe figs filled with *mascarpone* cheese. (Pictured below.)

8   ounces hot Italian sausages, cut in half crosswise
2   tablespoons plus ½ cup dry white wine

1   tablespoon olive oil
1   medium onion, chopped
1   small red bell pepper, chopped
1½  tablespoons chopped fresh thyme
1   15- to16-ounce can small white beans or cannellini (white kidney beans), rinsed, drained
1   bunch fresh arugula

Place sausages in heavy medium skillet. Pierce each piece once with fork. Add 2 tablespoons wine. Cover and simmer over medium-low heat 5 minutes. Uncover, increase heat to medium-high and cook until sausages are brown and cooked through, turning occasionally, about 6 minutes. Transfer sausages to plate and slice thinly on diagonal.

Pour off all but 1 tablespoon drippings from skillet. Add oil and heat over medium-low heat. Add onion, red pepper and thyme and sauté until vegetables are slightly softened and brown, about 10 minutes. Increase heat to high, add remaining ½ cup wine and boil until reduced by half, stirring up any browned bits, about 3 minutes. Add beans and sausage and stir until heated through, about 3 minutes. Divide arugula between plates. Top with sausage mixture and serve.

# CHORIZO, PEPPER AND ONION SANDWICHES

2 SERVINGS; CAN BE DOUBLED

Garlicky chorizo sausage is one of our favorite additions to omelets, pizza and potato salad. It's especially delicious in this easy sandwich, which would be terrific after a bowl of refreshing gazpacho. A purchased flan or caramel custard would make an ideal finish.

| | |
|---|---|
| 1 | tablespoon olive oil |
| 8 | ounces fully cooked Spanish link chorizo sausage or other garlic sausage (such as kielbasa) |
| 1 | medium onion, thinly sliced |
| ½ | green bell pepper, thinly sliced |
| ½ | red bell pepper, thinly sliced |
| ½ | cup dry red wine |
| 2 | large rolls, split horizontally |

Heat oil in heavy large skillet over medium heat. Halve chorizo lengthwise. Add to skillet and cook until beginning to brown, turning occasionally, about 5 minutes. Transfer chorizo to plate. Cut crosswise into 2- to 3-inch pieces. Pour off all but 2 tablespoons fat. Add onion and bell peppers to skillet. Sauté until vegetables begin to soften, about 5 minutes. Return chorizo to skillet. Add wine and simmer to blend ingredients, stirring frequently, about 3 minutes. Season sausage mixture with salt and pepper. Place bottoms of rolls on 2 plates. Spoon sausage mixture over. Cover with tops of rolls and serve.

# SAUSAGE RATATOUILLE

2 SERVINGS; CAN BE DOUBLED

Crusty bread and something sweet — caramel ice cream sundaes — would round out this meal nicely.

| | |
|---|---|
| 1 | tablespoon olive oil |
| 8 | ounces hot Italian sausages, cut into 1-inch pieces |
| 3 | large Japanese eggplants, cut into 1-inch pieces |
| 1 | medium onion, thinly sliced |
| 1 | green bell pepper, thinly sliced |
| 8 | ounces tomatoes, cut into 1-inch pieces |
| ⅓ | cup coarsely chopped fresh basil or 1½ tablespoons dried, crumbled |

Heat oil in heavy large skillet over medium heat. Add sausages and sauté until brown, about 8 minutes. Using slotted spoon, transfer sausages to plate. Add eggplants, onion and bell pepper to skillet and sauté until beginning to soften, about 7 minutes. Return sausages to skillet; add tomatoes. Cover and simmer until vegetables are very tender, about 15 minutes. Mix in basil; season with salt and pepper. *(Can be prepared 1 day ahead. Cover and refrigerate. Reheat just until warm.)*

# MEATLESS

Whether you are a full-time vegetarian or, as more and more people do these days, simply enjoy enhancing your culinary repertoire with meatless meals, you'll find lots that's delectable in this chapter. We also guarantee it all quick and easy, not something we could have promised years back when vegetarian cooking was synonymous with time-consuming cooking. But the food industry has been listening, and supermarkets are now filled with products like canned beans that make preparing meatless dishes a breeze.

Take those beans, for example. Consumer demand has spawned entire new lines of different canned legumes, from shiny black beans to make Spicy Caribbean Black Beans (page 169) to white beans for zippy Cheese and Pinto Bean Quesadillas (page 171). Good-quality frozen black-eyed peas lend their nutty sweetness to an imaginative Black-eyed Pea and Feta Salad (page 164), and dried lentils, not new but newly discovered by many, appear in a lovely lemon-scented Lentil Stew with Spinach and Potatoes (page 161).

Delicious, quick-cooking grains create the foundations for some of the most exceptional dishes we know, among them creamy, cheesy Parmesan Polenta with Mushroom Marinara (page 175). Corn grits, another wonderful but often overlooked meatless staple, are transformed into a savory, down-home casserole of Baked Cheese Grits with Turnip Greens (page 162). Rice, both the regular and instant varieties, adds substance and texture to sophisticated dishes such as Risotto with Tomatoes and Roasted Garlic (page 178). Morocco's unique contribution to the quick cook's pantry is couscous, a semolina grain that "cooks" with just a five-minute soak in hot liquid. It's the

Tuscan Bread
Salad (page 159)

key player in a colorful and refreshing Greek-Style Couscous Salad (page 166).

Your supermarket's freezer case also yields up some excellent fast-cooking ingredients. Frozen vegetables are particularly useful, and form the basis of a sweetly spiced Gingered Squash Bisque with Sage Croutons (page 163), an easy Corn and Cheddar Chowder (page 169) and a soul-soothing Potato, Leek and Pea Soup (page 181).

Eggs, back in favor on the healthy foods list, are key to any number of meatless meals, from a potato-rich Tortilla Española (page 172) to a scrumptious Bell Pepper, Tomato and Cheese Omelet (page 166) to the inventive pairing of Baked Eggs in Corn

Grilled Eggplant
and Tomato
Sandwiches
(page 176)

Bread Stuffing (page 179). A choice selection of cheese dishes, among them a sensational Spinach, Brie and Walnut Salad (page 168), our streamlined version of a traditional Welsh favorite, Broccoli and Cheese Pasties (page 177) and an unctuous, comforting Stilton Rarebit (page 164), round out this tempting tour of meatless main courses.

# TUSCAN BREAD SALAD

2 SERVINGS; CAN BE DOUBLED

Begin with bowls of vichyssoise. Offer a variety of Italian olives alongside, and a purchased apricot tart for dessert. (Pictured on page 156.)

| | |
|---|---|
| 1 | pound tomatoes, chopped (about 2 large) |
| 1 | large yellow or red bell pepper, cut into ¾-inch pieces |
| 6 | ounces fresh mozzarella cheese, cut into ½-inch pieces |
| ⅓ | cup coarsely chopped fresh basil |
| 6 | tablespoons extra-virgin olive oil |
| 3 | tablespoons balsamic vinegar or red wine vinegar |
| 3 | garlic cloves, minced |
| 4 | ounces crusty Italian or French bread, cut into 1-inch cubes |
| | Fresh basil leaves (optional) |

Combine tomatoes, bell pepper, cheese and chopped basil in large bowl. Whisk oil, vinegar and garlic to blend in small bowl. Season to taste with salt and pepper. Pour dressing over salad and toss to coat well. *(Can be prepared 1 hour ahead. Let stand at room temperature.)*

Preheat broiler. Place bread on baking sheet and broil just until beginning to color, stirring once, about 1 minute. Add bread to salad and mix gently. Divide salad between 2 shallow bowls. Garnish with fresh basil leaves if desired and serve.

# QUICK SOUP AU PISTOU

2 SERVINGS; CAN BE DOUBLED

This rustic soup is chock-full of precut fresh vegetables. *Pistou* is a classic French sauce that is like Italian pesto without the pine nuts; purchased pesto works well in this dish. All this soup needs to become a meal is some bread and a tart from the bakery for dessert.

| | |
|---|---|
| 2 | 14½-ounce cans vegetable broth |
| 1 | 14- to 16-ounce can Italian-style stewed tomatoes |
| 2 | cups purchased mixed cut-up raw vegetables, such as broccoli, cauliflower, carrots and celery |
| 1 | 15- to 16-ounce can white beans (such as Great Northern), drained |
| 1 | ounce spaghetti, broken into 1-inch pieces (about ⅓ cup) |
| ¼ | cup purchased pesto sauce |

Bring broth and tomatoes with their juices to boil in heavy medium saucepan over high heat, breaking up tomatoes with back of spoon. Add 2 cups mixed vegetables. Reduce heat to medium-low. Cover pan and simmer soup 10 minutes. Add beans and pasta and cook, uncovered, until vegetables are tender and pasta is cooked through, about 10 minutes. Season soup to taste with salt and pepper.

Ladle soup into bowls; top with large spoonfuls of pesto.

# MEXICAN TORTILLA CASSEROLE

2 SERVINGS; CAN BE DOUBLED

For extra flavor, use the now easy-to-find Monterey Jack cheese with jalapeños. A grapefruit, red onion and sliced avocado salad makes a great accompaniment, and sugar cookies are a terrific ending to the meal.
(Pictured above.)

1    14½-ounce can Mexican-style stewed tomatoes
⅓    cup packed chopped fresh cilantro

5    6-inch corn tortillas
1½    cups packed grated Monterey Jack cheese (about 6 ounces)
      Sour cream (optional)
¼    cup sliced pitted black olives (optional)

Preheat oven to 450°F. Using on/off turns, puree tomatoes with their juices and ¼ cup cilantro in processor.

Spread ¼ cup sauce in bottom of 8-inch-diameter glass pie dish. Top with 1 tortilla. Sprinkle with ⅓ cup cheese. Spoon ¼ cup sauce over. Repeat layering 3 more times using 1 tortilla, ⅓ cup cheese and ¼ cup sauce for each layer. Top with remaining tortilla, sauce and cheese. Bake until cheese melts and sauce bubbles, about 10 minutes. Sprinkle with remaining cilantro. Garnish with sour cream and olives, if desired. Cut into wedges. Serve immediately.

# LENTIL STEW WITH SPINACH AND POTATOES

2 SERVINGS; CAN BE DOUBLED

Reflecting the cuisines of Israel and the surrounding Mediterranean Middle Eastern countries, this meatless stew is highly seasoned with mint and lemon. Sesame seed rolls or bread sticks, a tomato and cucumber salad and pistachio ice cream complete the meal.

| | |
|---|---|
| 2 | tablespoons olive oil |
| 2 | large garlic cloves, chopped |
| 3 | cups canned vegetable broth |
| 1 | cup lentils, rinsed, picked over |
| 8 | ounces red-skinned potatoes, cut into 1/2-inch pieces |
| 1 | lemon |
| 6 | ounces torn fresh spinach leaves (about 8 cups) |
| 1/4 | teaspoon cayenne pepper |
| 1/4 | cup chopped fresh mint |
| | Crumbled feta cheese (optional) |

Heat oil in heavy large saucepan over medium heat. Add garlic and stir 30 seconds. Add broth and lentils and bring to boil. Reduce heat, cover and simmer 10 minutes. Add potatoes and cook uncovered until potatoes and lentils are tender, stirring occasionally, 15 minutes.

Meanwhile, grate 1/2 teaspoon peel from lemon; squeeze enough juice from lemon to measure 2 tablespoons. Add lemon peel, lemon juice, spinach and cayenne pepper to stew. Cover and simmer until spinach wilts and is cooked through, about 2 minutes. Mix in mint. Season to taste with salt and pepper. *(Can be prepared 1 day ahead. Cover and refrigerate. Rewarm over low heat before serving.)* Spoon stew into large soup bowls. Sprinkle crumbled feta cheese over, if desired.

❧

# BAKED BEAN SOUP

2 SERVINGS; CAN BE DOUBLED

We use some of the traditional flavors of New England baked beans in this hearty dish. If you prefer a thicker soup, remove one cup of the beans, mash them to a paste, then stir them back into the soup. Coleslaw and corn bread squares round out the menu; a simple baked apple could be the perfect finale.

| | |
|---|---|
| 2 | tablespoons olive oil |
| 1 | large onion, chopped |
| 5 | teaspoons chili powder |
| 1 1/2 | teaspoons dry mustard |
| 2 | cups water |
| 2 | 15-ounce cans cannellini (white kidney beans), rinsed, drained |
| 1 | 14 1/2-ounce can stewed tomatoes with juices |
| 3 | tablespoons unsulfered (light) molasses |

Heat oil in heavy large saucepan over medium heat. Add onion and cook until soft, about 8 minutes. Add chili powder and mustard and stir 1 minute. Add water, beans, tomatoes with their juices and molasses. Simmer soup 15 minutes, stirring occasionally and breaking up large chunks of tomato with back of spoon. Season with salt and pepper.

# BAKED CHEESE GRITS WITH TURNIP GREENS

2 SERVINGS; CAN BE DOUBLED

Using frozen turnip greens saves time when making this vegetarian main course. It goes well with a carrot salad. Afterward, serve warm purchased gingerbread à la mode.

2      cups (about) salted water
⅔      cup quick-cooking grits

1      tablespoon butter
2      large garlic cloves, minced
3      cups frozen chopped turnip greens (about 10 ounces), thawed, squeezed dry

1¼     cups packed grated sharp cheddar cheese (about 5 ounces)
¼      teaspoon hot pepper sauce (such as Tabasco)

Position rack in center of oven and preheat to 375°F. Butter 4-cup soufflé dish. Bring 2 cups salted water to boil in heavy medium saucepan over high heat. Gradually whisk grits into water. Reduce heat to low. Cover and cook until grits are tender and mixture is thick, stirring occasionally and adding water if grits are very thick, 5 minutes.

Meanwhile, melt butter in heavy medium skillet over medium heat. Add garlic; sauté 1 minute. Add greens; stir 1 minute.

Mix greens and 1 cup cheese into grits. Add hot pepper sauce and season with salt and pepper. Transfer to prepared dish. Sprinkle remaining ¼ cup cheese over. *(Can be prepared 2 hours ahead. Let stand at room temperature.)* Bake until cheese melts and grits are heated through, about 15 minutes. Let stand 5 minutes and serve.

∾

# FIVE-SPICE VEGETABLE STIR-FRY

2 SERVINGS; CAN BE DOUBLED

The key to keeping this vegetarian entrée simple is to use precut packaged vegetables available in your market's produce section or salad bar. Serve rice alongside, and lemon frozen yogurt with fortune cookies for dessert.

8      ounces firm tofu (bean curd), cut into ¾-inch pieces (about half of 14-ounce package)
3      tablespoons vegetable oil

8      ounces mixed broccoli and cauliflower florets (about 3 cups)
4      ounces thinly sliced carrots (about 1 cup)
3      ounces snow peas, strings removed (about 1 cup packed)
3      large garlic cloves, chopped
⅓      cup canned vegetable broth or water
1      teaspoon five-spice powder
3      tablespoons soy sauce

Arrange tofu on double-thick layer of paper towels and drain well. Heat 2 tablespoons oil in heavy large skillet over high heat. Add tofu in single layer and fry 3 minutes until brown on bottom. Turn over tofu and fry 3 minutes. Transfer tofu to plate.

Heat 1 tablespoon oil in same skillet over high heat. Add broccoli, cauliflower and carrots; stir-fry 1 minute. Add snow peas and garlic; stir-fry 30 seconds. Add broth and five-spice powder. Cover skillet; cook until vegetables are crisp-tender, about 2 minutes. Add soy sauce and tofu; toss until heated through. Serve immediately.

# GINGERED SQUASH BISQUE WITH SAGE CROUTONS

2 SERVINGS; CAN BE DOUBLED

Offer rolls and a salad of chopped Belgian endive, cherry tomatoes and blue cheese to complement the soup. Brownies à la mode are a luscious finale. (Pictured below.)

2½ cups (or more) canned vegetable broth
1 pound russet potatoes (about 2 large), peeled, finely chopped
1 12-ounce package frozen cooked orange-fleshed (winter) squash
1 teaspoon ground ginger

2½ tablespoons butter
1 large leek (white and pale green parts only), finely chopped

1 cup half and half

2 slices whole wheat bread, cubed
1½ teaspoons dried rubbed sage

Combine 2½ cups broth, potatoes, squash and ginger in heavy medium saucepan over medium-high heat. Cover and cook until potatoes are tender, about 10 minutes. Transfer to processor and puree.

Meanwhile, melt 1 tablespoon butter in large saucepan over low heat. Add leek. Cover and cook until tender, stirring often, 8 minutes.

Add vegetable puree and half and half to leek and simmer 2 minutes, thinning with additional broth, if desired. Season soup to taste with salt and pepper. *(Soup can be prepared 1 day ahead. Cover and refrigerate. Rewarm before continuing.)*

Melt remaining 1½ tablespoons butter in heavy small skillet over medium heat. Add bread cubes and sage and sauté until bread is toasted, about 3 minutes. Ladle soup into bowls. Sprinkle croutons over.

## STILTON RAREBIT

2 SERVINGS; CAN BE DOUBLED

Roquefort is an excellent substitute for the Stilton, or use the traditional well-aged cheddar. Serve with a salad of fresh mixed greens, and end with fruitcake and sliced fresh oranges.

1½ tablespoons butter
1½ tablespoons all purpose flour
1 teaspoon dry mustard (preferably Colman's)
1½ cups milk
1 cup packed crumbled Stilton cheese (about 4 ounces)
1½ teaspoons (or more) Worcestershire sauce

4 slices whole wheat bread, toasted
1 small green onion, finely chopped

Melt butter in heavy medium saucepan over medium heat. Whisk in flour. Cook 30 seconds. Whisk in mustard. Gradually whisk in milk. Bring to boil, whisking constantly. Reduce heat to medium-low and simmer until sauce thickens, whisking occasionally, about 8 minutes. Remove from heat. Add half of cheese and whisk until melted. Add remaining cheese; whisk until melted and smooth. Season with Worcestershire sauce, salt and pepper. *(Can be prepared 1 day ahead; chill. Whisk over low heat until heated through before continuing.)*

Cut toast in half diagonally and overlap 4 halves on each of 2 plates. Ladle rarebit over. Garnish with onion.

## BLACK-EYED PEA AND FETA SALAD

2 SERVINGS; CAN BE DOUBLED

Corn bread or corn muffins go well with this salad; purchased pecan pie is an appropriately southern finale. (Pictured on page 112.)

¼ cup chopped drained oil-packed sun-dried tomatoes
2 teaspoons Dijon mustard
2 teaspoons honey
3 tablespoons balsamic vinegar or red wine vinegar
¼ cup olive oil

1 10-ounce package frozen black-eyed peas, cooked according to package directions, drained
1 red bell pepper, diced
½ cup thinly sliced green onions
1 cup crumbled feta cheese (about 4 ounces)

3 cups mixed baby greens or bite-size pieces romaine lettuce

Combine sun-dried tomatoes, mustard and honey in small bowl. Whisk in vinegar, then oil. Season dressing with salt and pepper. *(Can be prepared 4 hours ahead. Let stand at room temperature.)*

Combine black-eyed peas, bell pepper and green onions in medium bowl. Toss with enough dressing to season to taste. Mix in feta.

Divide greens between 2 plates. Mound salad on greens. Serve, passing any extra dressing separately.

# SAFFRON RISOTTO PRIMAVERA

2 SERVINGS; CAN BE DOUBLED

Start the meal with artichokes filled with a lemon mayonnaise for dipping, and serve the risotto with a mixed-green and cherry tomato salad and a basket of toasted herb bread. To polish things off, set out a purchased raspberry tart. (Pictured below.)

| | |
|---|---|
| 3 | cups canned vegetable broth |
| 8 | ounces slender asparagus, ends trimmed, cut into 1-inch pieces |
| 1 | cup dry white wine |
| ¼ | teaspoon saffron threads |
| 1½ | tablespoons olive oil |
| 1 | cup arborio rice or medium-grain white rice |
| 1 | cup frozen petit peas, thawed |
| ⅓ | cup grated Parmesan cheese (about 1 ounce) |

Bring broth to boil in heavy medium saucepan. Add asparagus and cook until crisp-tender, about 2 minutes. Using slotted spoon, transfer to bowl. Add wine and saffron to broth and bring to simmer.

Heat oil in another heavy medium saucepan over medium heat. Add rice and stir until translucent, about 2 minutes. Mix in all but ¼ cup broth mixture. Simmer rice uncovered until tender and creamy, but still firm to bite, stirring occasionally, about 20 minutes. Mix in peas, then asparagus and cheese. Add remaining ¼ cup broth if risotto seems dry. Season to taste with salt and pepper and serve.

## Bell Pepper, Tomato and Cheese Omelet

2 SERVINGS; CAN BE DOUBLED

This recipe yields two individual omelets, but you can also make one big omelet in a large skillet and cut it in half. Serve the omelet with a spinach and orange salad and french fries, and finish with pecan sweet rolls and espresso. (Pictured at right.)

2   tablespoons olive oil
1   small onion, chopped
1   small green bell pepper, chopped
2   tomatoes, seeded, chopped
1   teaspoon dried oregano, crumbled
    Large pinch of cayenne pepper

4   eggs
1   tablespoon water
½   cup grated Fontina or Monterey Jack cheese
4   tablespoons grated Parmesan cheese

Heat 1½ tablespoons oil in heavy medium nonstick skillet over medium heat. Add onion and bell pepper; sauté until almost soft, about 5 minutes. Add tomatoes, oregano and cayenne and simmer until vegetables are very soft and filling is thick, about 3 minutes. Season with salt and pepper. Transfer filling to small bowl; do not wash skillet.

Whisk eggs and 1 tablespoon water in small bowl until well blended. Mix in ¼ cup Fontina cheese. Season with salt and pepper. Heat same skillet over medium-high heat. Pour in half of egg mixture and stir with back of fork until eggs begin to set. Cook until mixture is set, lifting edges occasionally with spatula to let uncooked egg run under, about 2 minutes. Spoon half of filling, half of remaining Fontina and 2 tablespoons Parmesan into center. Fold sides over filling to enclose. Turn out onto plate. Cover with foil. Add remaining ½ tablespoon oil to skillet. Repeat with remaining egg, filling and cheeses.

## Greek-Style Couscous Salad

2 SERVINGS; CAN BE DOUBLED

This salad is attractive on romaine lettuce leaves, and warm pita bread is perfect on the side. To complete the meal, serve poached apricots with scoops of vanilla frozen yogurt.

⅔   cup couscous
1   cup boiling water

¾   cup canned garbanzo beans (chick-peas), drained
½   cup chopped yellow or red bell pepper
⅓   cup sliced pitted black olives (preferably imported)
⅓   cup chopped red onion
3   tablespoons chopped fresh mint
3   tablespoons olive oil
2   tablespoons fresh lemon juice
¾   cup crumbled feta cheese (about 3 ounces)

Place couscous in medium bowl. Pour 1 cup boiling water over and stir to combine. Set aside until couscous is soft and water is absorbed, about 10 minutes. Fluff couscous with fork.

Add garbanzo beans, bell pepper, olives, onion and mint and toss. Mix in olive oil and lemon juice, then feta cheese. Season to taste with salt and pepper. Refrigerate until ready to serve.

# SPINACH, BRIE AND WALNUT SALAD

2 SERVINGS; CAN BE DOUBLED

Cheese-topped toasts add crunch to
this salad, which is great served with a
bowl of cream of tomato soup to begin,
and sliced peaches drizzled with
amaretto to finish.
(Pictured above.)

¼  cup olive oil
1½  tablespoons white wine vinegar
8  cups spinach leaves (about 6 ounces), torn into bite-size pieces
½  cup thinly sliced red onion
6  ounces Brie cheese, diced, room temperature

2  sandwich-size French bread slices

½  cup toasted walnut pieces

Whisk oil and vinegar to blend in small bowl. Season dressing
to taste with salt and pepper. Combine spinach, onion and half of cheese
in large bowl. Set salad aside.

Preheat broiler. Divide remaining cheese between bread slices.
Broil until cheese melts, about 1 minute. Cut toasts diagonally in half.

Toss salad with enough dressing to coat well. Divide salad between 2 plates. Sprinkle with walnuts. Arrange 2 toast halves at edge of
each salad and serve immediately.

## CORN AND CHEDDAR CHOWDER

2 GENEROUS SERVINGS; CAN BE DOUBLED

Whole grain bread and a salad of mixed greens, marinated artichoke hearts and roasted peppers would be great with this soup. Finish with fresh fruit.

| | |
|---|---|
| 1 | tablespoon unsalted butter |
| 1 | onion, chopped |
| ¾ | pound red-skinned potatoes, peeled, diced |
| 2 | cups frozen corn kernels |
| 2 | cups half and half or milk |
| 1 | cup (or more) canned vegetable broth |
| 1½ | teaspoons dried thyme, crumbled |
| 2 | cups grated medium-sharp cheddar cheese (about 6 ounces) |

Melt butter in heavy medium saucepan over medium-high heat. Add onion; sauté until tender, about 5 minutes. Add potatoes, corn, half and half, 1 cup broth and thyme. Cover pan partially; simmer chowder until potatoes are tender, about 15 minutes. (*Can be prepared 1 day ahead. Chill. Before continuing, rewarm over low heat, thinning with more broth if desired.*) Add cheese; stir until melted. Season to taste with salt and pepper and serve immediately.

∾

## SPICY CARIBBEAN BLACK BEANS

4 SERVINGS; CAN BE DOUBLED

Offer buttered, grilled Cuban (or French) bread with the beans. Splash rum and grenadine over tropical fruits for a colorful finale.

| | |
|---|---|
| ¼ | cup olive oil |
| 1 | large onion, chopped |
| 2 | large garlic cloves, chopped |
| 1½ | teaspoons chili powder |
| 2 | 15- to 16-ounce cans black beans, well drained |
| 3 | cups water |
| 1 | bay leaf |
| 1 | tablespoon red wine vinegar |
| ½ | teaspoon hot pepper sauce (such as Tabasco) |
| | Pinch of sugar |
| | |
| 1 | cup long-grain white rice |
| ½ | teaspoon turmeric |
| | |
| ¾ | cup chopped red onion |
| 2 | jalapeño chilies, seeded, minced |
| ½ | 7-ounce jar roasted red peppers, drained, thinly sliced |

Heat oil in heavy large saucepan over medium heat. Add onion and cook until softened, about 5 minutes. Add garlic and chili powder and cook 1 minute, stirring. Add beans, 1 cup water and bay leaf. Simmer until thick soup consistency, 20 minutes. Remove bay leaf. Add vinegar, pepper sauce and sugar. Season with salt and pepper.

Meanwhile, bring remaining 2 cups water to boil in heavy medium saucepan. Add rice, turmeric and salt and stir. Cover and cook over low heat until all liquid is absorbed, 20 minutes.

Mix chopped red onion and chilies in small bowl. Mound rice in center of platter. Spoon beans around rice. Arrange roasted pepper slices atop beans. Pass red onion relish separately.

# PESTO POTATO CAKE WITH TOMATO SAUCE

2 SERVINGS; CAN BE DOUBLED

If you don't have leftover mashed potatoes, boil 1½ pounds peeled russet potatoes until tender; drain. Mash with ¼ cup milk or broth and one tablespoon butter, then season with salt and pepper. A cucumber and red-onion salad with crisp breadsticks is a great opener, and homemade hot fudge sundaes would be a family-pleasing dessert. (Pictured below.)

2½  tablespoons olive oil
1   medium-large zucchini, cut into ½-inch cubes
1   large garlic clove, chopped
1   14½-ounce can Italian-style stewed tomatoes with juices

3   cups leftover mashed potatoes, room temperature
1   egg
3   tablespoons purchased pesto sauce

Heat 2 tablespoons oil in heavy medium skillet over medium-high heat. Add zucchini and sauté until beginning to brown, about 5 minutes. Add garlic and cook 1 minute. Mix in tomatoes. Reduce heat to medium and simmer until zucchini is tender and sauce thickens slightly, breaking up tomatoes with back of spoon, about 8 minutes. Season to taste with salt and pepper. *(Can be prepared 1 day ahead. Cover and refrigerate. Rewarm before using.)*

Preheat oven to 475°F. Brush 8-inch-diameter cake pan with ½ tablespoon oil. Mix mashed potatoes and egg in medium bowl until well blended. Spread half of potato mixture in prepared pan. Spread half of pesto over. Repeat layering with potatoes and pesto.

Bake potato cake until heated through and light brown on top, about 15 minutes. Let stand 5 minutes. Cut cake into wedges or spoon out onto plates. Spoon tomato-zucchini sauce alongside and serve.

## CHEESE AND PINTO BEAN QUESADILLAS

2 SERVINGS; CAN BE DOUBLED

A fun-to-eat vegetarian entrée. Add your favorite guacamole, purchased salsa and a jicama and romaine salad. Old-fashioned ice cream sandwiches would make dessert fun, too.

2   cups packed grated hot pepper Monterey Jack cheese (about 8 ounces)
2   teaspoons chili powder
1   15- to 16-ounce can pinto beans, rinsed, drained
⅓   cup chopped onion
⅓   cup chopped fresh cilantro

4   8-inch-diameter flour tortillas

Preheat oven to 375°F. Toss cheese and chili powder in large bowl until well blended. Add beans, onion and cilantro and toss.

Arrange 2 tortillas on baking sheet. Press half of cheese filling over each tortilla, leaving ¾-inch border at edges. Firmly press second tortilla atop each. Bake until cheese melts and filling is heated through, about 10 minutes. Cut each quesadilla into 6 wedges.

## FRIED RICE WITH VEGETABLES

2 SERVINGS; CAN BE DOUBLED

Serve this with a salad of snow peas, radishes and Boston lettuce, and finish with grapes and fortune cookies. If you double the recipe, make two egg "pancakes" in two batches.

4   tablespoons peanut oil
1   egg
2   teaspoons water

1¼   cups sliced fresh shiitake or button mushrooms
1¼   cups small broccoli florets
1¼   cups chopped red bell pepper
1½   tablespoons minced peeled fresh ginger
1¼   cups thinly sliced green onions (about 5)
3   cups cold cooked long-grain white rice (about 1 cup uncooked)
3   tablespoons soy sauce
  Additional soy sauce

Heat 1 tablespoon oil in heavy large nonstick skillet over medium heat. Beat egg with water until well blended. Pour into skillet, tilting to spread egg to thin 10-inch round. Cook until golden and flecked with brown spots, about 1 minute. Release edges and turn "pancake" over. Cook until second side is done, 30 seconds. Transfer egg pancake to work surface and cut into ½-inch-wide 2-inch-long strips.

Heat remaining 3 tablespoons oil in same skillet over high heat. Add mushrooms, broccoli, red pepper and ginger. Stir until vegetables are just tender, about 3 minutes. Add green onions and cook 1 minute longer. Add rice and 3 tablespoons soy sauce to skillet. Cook until mixture is thoroughly blended and heated through, stirring almost constantly. Mix in egg strips and season generously with pepper. Divide fried rice between plates and serve, passing additional soy sauce.

# Southwest Vegetable Ragout

2 SERVINGS; CAN BE DOUBLED

Team this up with a chicory and red-onion salad with blue-cheese vinaigrette, corn bread and rice pilaf for a balanced vegetarian meal. Top it all off with chocolate frozen yogurt drizzled with a little coffee liqueur.

1   large red potato, cut into ½-inch pieces
3   tablespoons olive oil
1   medium-size green bell pepper, cut into ½-inch pieces
2   large garlic cloves, chopped
1   tablespoon chili powder
1   14½-ounce can Mexican-style stewed tomatoes
1   cup frozen corn kernels
1   15- to 16-ounce can black beans, rinsed, drained
2   tablespoons minced fresh cilantro

Cook potato in small pot of boiling salted water until almost tender, about 8 minutes. Drain and reserve.

Meanwhile, heat oil in heavy large saucepan over medium heat. Add green pepper and sauté 3 minutes. Add garlic and chili powder and stir 1 minute. Add tomatoes with their juices, corn, beans, cilantro and reserved potato. Simmer until potato is very tender and liquids are thick, stirring occasionally, about 10 minutes. Season with salt and pepper.

# Tortilla Española

2 SERVINGS; CAN BE DOUBLED

If anything can lay claim to being the national dish of Spain, it is *tortilla*. It's served at room temperature in every *tapas* bar in Spain, although we present ours warm. You can add crusty whole wheat rolls and a salad of spring greens as accompaniments, then follow with fruit tartlets. If you double the recipe, make two *tortillas,* keeping the first one warm in a 200°F oven.

4   tablespoons olive oil
1   pound red potatoes, thinly sliced
1   medium onion, thinly sliced

4   eggs
    Chopped fresh parsley

Heat 3 tablespoons oil in heavy medium nonstick skillet over medium-low heat. Layer potatoes and onion in skillet, seasoning each layer with salt and pepper. Cover and cook until vegetables are tender, turning once, about 15 minutes. Cool 5 minutes. *(Can be prepared 2 hours ahead. Let stand at room temperature.)*

Beat eggs to blend in medium bowl. Add potato mixture and mix well. Heat same skillet over medium-low heat. Add remaining 1 tablespoon oil. Pour egg mixture into skillet. Cook until bottom is just golden and top is still unset, occasionally lifting edges of omelet with spatula and tilting pan to let uncooked egg run underneath, about 5 minutes. Loosen eggs and slide onto large plate. Invert plate, returning eggs cooked side up to skillet, and cook until eggs are fully set, about 3 minutes longer. Cut tortilla into wedges. Garnish with parsley.

# Swiss Fondue with Vegetables

2 SERVINGS; CAN BE DOUBLED

We suggest setting out boiled baby red-skinned potatoes, blanched broccoli florets and chunks of crusty French bread to dip into the fondue. A spinach, pear and walnut salad tossed with warm vinaigrette makes a sophisticated start, and an apple tart is a nice finish. (Pictured above.)

8 ounces Swiss cheese (such as Emmenthal or Gruyère), grated
1½ tablespoons all purpose flour
⅛ teaspoon ground nutmeg
¾ cup dry white wine
1 garlic clove, minced

2 tablespoons kirsch (clear cherry brandy)
Boiled baby red-skinned potatoes
Blanched broccoli florets
French bread, cubed

Toss cheese with flour and nutmeg in medium bowl. Bring wine and garlic to simmer in heavy medium saucepan over low heat. Add cheese by handfuls, using whisk to stir constantly and allowing each addition to melt before adding next. Continue to stir until fondue is almost smooth and blended, about 3 minutes. *(Can be prepared 1 hour ahead. Cover and let stand. Rewarm over low heat, stirring often.)*

Add kirsch and stir until fondue is smooth. Season to taste with pepper. Serve with potatoes, broccoli and bread.

# Black Bean Salad with Artichokes and Red Pepper

2 SERVINGS; CAN BE DOUBLED

A big basket of crusty bread would go well with this salad. For dessert: angel food cake topped with strawberries. (Pictured at left.)

| | |
|---|---|
| 1 | 15- to 16-ounce can black beans, rinsed, drained |
| ⅔ | cup chopped red bell pepper |
| ½ | cup chopped sweet yellow onion (such as Maui or Vidalia) |
| 1 | 6-ounce jar marinated artichoke hearts |
| | |
| 1 | bunch fresh arugula |
| 2 | ounces soft mild goat cheese (such as Montrachet), crumbled |

Combine beans, bell pepper and onion in medium bowl. Stir in artichokes with marinade. Season with salt and pepper.

Arrange 1 bunch arugula on 2 plates. Spoon black bean salad atop arugula. Sprinkle 2 ounces crumbled goat cheese over each salad and then serve salads immediately.

# Parmesan Polenta with Mushroom Marinara

2 SERVINGS; CAN BE DOUBLED

Serve this microwaveable main course with a Caesar salad and hot garlic bread, then drizzle anise liqueur over lemon sherbet for a refreshing finale.

| | |
|---|---|
| 2 | tablespoons olive oil |
| 5 | ounces button mushrooms, thinly sliced |
| 1 | 14-ounce jar marinara or herb pasta sauce |
| ½ | cup dry red wine |
| ⅛ | teaspoon dried crushed red pepper |
| ¼ | cup chopped fresh parsley |
| | |
| 2 | cups water |
| ½ | cup plus 2 tablespoons yellow cornmeal |
| ¼ | teaspoon salt |
| ½ | cup packed grated mozzarella cheese (about 2 ounces) |
| ½ | cup grated Parmesan cheese (about 1½ ounces) |

Additional Parmesan cheese

Heat olive oil in heavy medium skillet over medium-high heat. Add sliced mushrooms and sauté until beginning to soften and brown, about 5 minutes. Add marinara sauce, red wine and crushed red pepper. Simmer until sauce thickens slightly, about 15 minutes. *(Can be prepared 1 day ahead. Cover and refrigerate. Reheat sauce before continuing.)* Mix in chopped fresh parsley.

Whisk water, cornmeal and salt together until blended in large microwave-safe bowl. Cover and cook on High 5 minutes. Whisk polenta until smooth. Re-cover and cook 3 minutes longer. Let stand 1 minute. Whisk in ½ cup mozzarella cheese and ½ cup Parmesan cheese; season polenta to taste with salt and pepper.

Divide polenta between two plates. Spoon sauce over. Serve, passing additional Parmesan separately.

# GRILLED EGGPLANT AND TOMATO SANDWICHES

2 SERVINGS; CAN BE DOUBLED

A wonderful smoky flavor permeates these sandwiches. If your grill has no cover, tent foil over the sandwiches to melt the cheese. Begin with a romaine salad, and offer chocolate-covered coffee ice cream bars for a casual finale. (Pictured below.)

3 large Japanese eggplants, each cut lengthwise into thirds
⅓ cup olive oil
2 large garlic cloves, minced
¼ cup chopped fresh basil plus 8 large fresh basil leaves
4 ½-inch-thick diagonal slices country-style bread
1 large tomato, cut into ¼-inch-thick slices

4 slices Fontina cheese
Fresh basil sprigs

Prepare barbecue (medium-high heat). Sprinkle eggplant slices generously with salt. Let stand 5 minutes. Pat dry. Combine oil, garlic and chopped basil in small bowl. Season with salt and pepper. Brush eggplant slices, bread and tomato slices with garlic oil.

Grill eggplant until very tender and slightly charred, turning frequently, about 7 minutes per side. Arrange bread and tomatoes on barbecue during last 3 minutes of eggplant-grilling time and cook until bread is golden and tomatoes begin to soften, about 1 minute per side.

Transfer 2 bread slices to plate. Top each remaining bread slice on grill with eggplant, cheese, tomato slices and whole basil leaves, dividing evenly. Season with salt and pepper. Cover grill until cheese just melts, about 1 minute. Transfer sandwiches to plates. Top with second bread slices. Garnish with basil sprigs and serve.

# CHUNKY VEGETABLE STEW

2 SERVINGS; CAN BE DOUBLED

Tomatoes, sweet potato, chick-peas and zucchini simmer in a garlicky tomato sauce to make a satisfying meatless main dish. Begin with a light salad of crisp cucumber slices tossed with a dill vinaigrette. Buttered couscous makes a great side dish. Serve pound cake topped with chocolate ice cream and hot fudge sauce for a quick dessert.

| | |
|---|---|
| ¼ | cup olive oil |
| 1 | onion, thickly sliced |
| 2 | large garlic cloves, chopped |
| 1 | 14½-ounce can stewed tomatoes with juices |
| 1 | 8-ounce sweet potato, peeled, cut into ½-inch pieces |
| 1 | cup drained canned garbanzo beans (chick-peas) |
| ¾ | teaspoon dried rosemary, crumbled |
| 1 | medium zucchini, cut into ½-inch-thick rounds |
| ¼ | cup grated Parmesan cheese |

Heat olive oil in heavy large saucepan over medium heat. Add sliced onion and cook until slightly softened, separating slices into rings, about 5 minutes. Add garlic and cook 1 minute. Add tomatoes with their juices, sweet potato, garbanzo beans and rosemary. Bring mixture to simmer, stirring occasionally. Cover and cook 5 minutes. Add zucchini. Cover and cook until sweet potato is tender, about 15 minutes. Season to taste with salt and pepper. Divide stew between soup bowls. Top with Parmesan cheese and then serve.

# BROCCOLI AND CHEESE PASTIES

2 SERVINGS; CAN BE DOUBLED

The "a" in the name for these palm-size pies is pronounced as in "past." They became popular in Cornwall as a portable lunch for workers and schoolchildren. Partnered with tomato soup and a fruit salad, they make a quick supper. Sprinkle raspberries and crumbled brandy snaps over ice cream for a simple dessert.

| | |
|---|---|
| 1 | large bunch broccoli, cut into florets |
| 1½ | cups packed grated sharp cheddar cheese (about 6 ounces) |
| ½ | cup thinly sliced green onions |
| 1½ | tablespoons chopped fresh dill or 1½ teaspoons dried dillweed |
| ¼ | teaspoon ground nutmeg |
| 1 | 15-ounce package All Ready Pie Crusts, room temperature |
| 1 | egg beaten with 1 tablespoon water (for glaze) |

Preheat oven to 400°F. Steam broccoli until crisp-tender. Cool. Combine 2 cups florets with next 4 ingredients in medium bowl. Season filling with pepper and toss to combine.

Unfold crusts on work surface. Press out fold lines if necessary. Cut each crust in half, creating 4 half circles. Mound ¼ of filling on half of each pastry; press filling to compact. Brush pastry edges with glaze. Fold second half of each pastry over filling, pressing to seal edges and forming triangle. Using tines of fork, crimp pastry edges. Pierce pasties several times with tines of fork.

Place pasties on large baking sheet; brush generously with glaze. Bake pasties until golden brown, about 22 minutes..

# RISOTTO WITH TOMATOES AND ROASTED GARLIC

2 SERVINGS; CAN BE DOUBLED

This flavorful dish could be preceded by a salad of roasted peppers and followed by assorted *biscotti* with sliced peaches.

|     |                                                        |
| --- | ------------------------------------------------------ |
| 5   | garlic cloves, unpeeled                                |
| 2½  | tablespoons olive oil                                  |
| 3   | cups canned vegetable broth                            |
| 1   | cup dry white wine                                     |
| 1   | cup arborio rice or medium-grain white rice (about 7 ounces) |
| 2   | cups chopped seeded tomatoes                           |
| ⅔   | cup sliced fresh basil                                 |
| ⅓   | cup grated Parmesan cheese                             |

Preheat oven to 450°F. Place unpeeled garlic cloves on small sheet of foil. Drizzle garlic with ½ tablespoon oil and enclose in foil. Roast garlic cloves until soft, about 20 minutes.

Meanwhile, pour broth and wine into heavy medium saucepan. Bring to simmer. Heat remaining 2 tablespoons oil in another medium saucepan over medium heat. Add rice to oil and stir until translucent, about 2 minutes. Add all but ¼ cup broth mixture to rice. Cook until rice is tender but still slightly firm to bite and mixture is creamy, stirring occasionally, approximately 20 minutes.

Squeeze roasted garlic out of skins onto foil and mash with fork, incorporating oil. Add garlic to rice. Stir in remaining ¼ cup broth if risotto seems dry; cook 1 minute. Add tomatoes, basil and cheese and stir until cheese melts. Serve immediately.

❧

# FOUR-HERB OMELET

2 SERVINGS; CAN BE DOUBLED

We've used a quartet of classic herbs in this simple and light French omelet. But feel free to vary them to suit your fancy. Great accompaniments would be fried potato slices and a mixed lettuce salad. End with macaroons and strawberries.

|     |                                                        |
| --- | ------------------------------------------------------ |
| 6   | eggs                                                   |
| 4   | teaspoons water                                        |
| 2   | teaspoons chopped fresh parsley                        |
| 2   | teaspoons chopped fresh chives                         |
| 2   | teaspoons chopped fresh tarragon or ½ teaspoon dried, crumbled |
| 2   | teaspoons chopped fresh thyme or ½ teaspoon dried, crumbled |
| 4   | teaspoons butter                                       |
|     | Whole fresh chives (optional)                          |

Whisk eggs and water in medium bowl to blend. Season with salt and pepper. Mix in parsley, chopped chives, tarragon and thyme. Melt 2 teaspoons butter in 8-inch omelet pan or heavy small skillet over high heat. Add half of eggs to pan and stir briefly. Let eggs begin to set around edges. Lift edges and tilt pan, letting uncooked portion flow under cooked eggs. Cook until eggs are almost set but still slightly moist, about 30 seconds. Using spatula as aid, roll ⅓ of omelet to center. Tilt pan; slide omelet onto plate while folding over second ⅓. Make second omelet with remaining butter and eggs. Garnish with whole chives.

# BAKED EGGS IN CORN BREAD STUFFING

2 SERVINGS; CAN BE DOUBLED

You can try any type of leftover stuffing in this dish. Accompany the entrée with steamed green beans and a salad of spinach and sliced red apples, and serve lemon sorbet for dessert.
(Pictured above.)

3  cups cooked stuffing
   Canned chicken or vegetable broth (optional)
4  eggs
⅓  cup grated Swiss cheese
2  tablespoons chopped green onions

Preheat oven to 350°F. Generously butter 2 shallow 1-cup gratin dishes. If stuffing is dry, place in small bowl and mix in enough broth by tablespoonfuls to moisten. Divide stuffing between prepared dishes, spreading to edge with back of spoon. Using back of spoon, make 2 deep hollows for eggs in stuffing in each dish. Carefully break eggs into hollows and sprinkle with cheese. Bake uncovered until cheese melts, egg whites are set and yolks move only slightly when dishes are gently shaken, about 18 minutes. Garnish eggs with chopped green onions. Season with pepper and serve.

# NEOCLASSIC GREEK SALAD

2 SERVINGS; CAN BE DOUBLED

Warm pita bread complements this salad. Purchased baklava, apricots and strong coffee would round it all out .

5 tablespoons olive oil
2½ tablespoons fresh lemon juice
1 teaspoon dried oregano, crumbled

4 cups torn romaine lettuce leaves (about ½ head)
1 cup thinly sliced red onion
¾ cup crumbled feta cheese (about 3 ounces)
1 small zucchini, trimmed, thinly sliced
8 cherry tomatoes
8 brine-cured black olives (such as Kalamata)

Whisk 5 tablespoons olive oil, 2½ tablespoons fresh lemon juice and 1 teaspoon oregano in small bowl to blend. Season dressing to taste with salt and pepper. *(Dressing can be prepared up to 1 day ahead. Cover with plastic and let stand at room temperature.)*

Toss lettuce with half of dressing in medium bowl to combine. Mound lettuce on 2 plates. Arrange onion, feta cheese, zucchini, tomatoes and olives over, dividing evenly. Drizzle remaining dressing over.

# SPINACH AND GRUYÈRE OMELET

2 SERVINGS; CAN BE DOUBLED

Dinner rolls and a sliced beet and cucumber salad are good with this main course. Offer sugar cookies, fresh green grapes and coffee for dessert.

3 teaspoons butter
1 small onion, chopped
2 tablespoons Dijon mustard
1 10-ounce package frozen chopped spinach, thawed, squeezed dry

4 eggs
¼ teaspoon ground nutmeg
1 cup packed grated Gruyère cheese

Melt 2 teaspoons butter in heavy medium skillet over medium heat. Add onion; sauté until soft and beginning to brown, about 10 minutes. Mix in mustard, then spinach. Season filling with salt and pepper; stir until heated through. *(Can be made 2 hours ahead. Let stand at room temperature. Rewarm filling before using.)*

Preheat broiler. Beat eggs and nutmeg in small bowl to blend. Mix in half of cheese. Melt remaining 1 teaspoon butter in medium nonstick skillet over medium-high heat. Pour egg mixture into skillet and cook until almost set in center, occasionally lifting edges and letting uncooked egg mixture flow underneath, about 4 minutes. Spoon filling over half of omelet; fold other half over. Sprinkle remaining cheese over omelet. Broil until cheese melts, about 1 minute.

# POTATO, LEEK AND PEA SOUP

2 SERVINGS; CAN BE DOUBLED

Sautéed leeks, croutons and a few peas make a pretty garnish for this lovely pale green soup. We like to serve it with French rolls, a salad of cherry tomatoes and baby greens, and a fresh fruit tart from the bakery to finish. (Pictured below.)

2   tablespoons (¼ stick) unsalted butter
1   large leek (white and pale green parts only), thinly sliced
1   large russet potato, peeled, thinly sliced (about 12 ounces)
1   14½-ounce can vegetable broth
1   cup frozen peas
½   teaspoon dried tarragon
¾   cup milk
    Ground white pepper

2   ½-inch-thick slices French bread, trimmed, cut into ½-inch cubes
2   tablespoons chopped fresh chives or green onions

Melt 1 tablespoon butter in heavy large saucepan over medium heat. Add leek and cook until tender, stirring occasionally, about 5 minutes. Add potato and broth and bring to boil. Reduce heat; cover and simmer 10 minutes. Add peas and tarragon and cook until peas and potatoes are tender, about 5 minutes. Puree soup in blender in batches. Return soup to pot; add milk. Bring soup to simmer. Season soup to taste with white pepper and salt.

Melt remaining 1 tablespoon butter in heavy small skillet over medium heat. Add bread cubes and sauté 3 minutes. Add chopped chives and sauté until bread is lightly toasted, about 2 minutes. Ladle soup into bowls. Top with croutons and serve.

# INDEX

Sautéed Sea
Scallops with
Lemon Dill Sauce
(page 110)

# ACKNOWLEDGMENTS

Chapter introductions and recipes by Brooke Dojny and Melanie Barnard.

Additional recipes provided by:
Linda Archer
Leah Balk
Sharmi Banik
Lena Cederham Birnbaum
Café Roma, San Luis Obispo, California
Susie Campbell
Maura Chamberlain
Stephanie Coon
Lane Crowther
Joseph D'Amore
Darren DiPietro
Beryl Edwards
Iris Erlingsdottir
Mark Flemming
Jessica Hirschman
Dianne Jefferies
Karen Kaplan
Jeanne Thiel Kelley
Kristine Kidd
Arlene Krieger
Bruce Landon
Carmela M. Meely
Bev Michaels
Selma Brown Morrow
Lisa Nesselson
Carol O'Gorman
Marilou Robinson
Richard Sax
Deborah Serangeli
Marie Simmons
Sarah Tenaglia
Susan Tollefson
Glenn Weber
Jason Williams
Cynthia Wilson

The following people contributed the photographs included in this book:
Peter Ardito
Ed Carey
Jennifer Cheung
Michael Deuson
Alison Duke
John Reed Forsman
Dennis Galante
Beth Galton
Dennis M. Gottlieb
Kari Haavisto
Henry Hamamoto
Charles Imstepf
Martin Jacobs
Robert Jacobs
Michael Lamotte
Lannen/Kelly
Ann Mitchell
Linda Okamura
Kathryn Russell
Glenn David Smith
Laurie Vogt
E. K. Waller

Original photography for this book and the front jacket were done by Dennis M. Gottlieb. Prop styling for these photographs: Adrienne Abseck. Food styling: Delores Custer. Food stylist assistant: Fred Thompson. Food stylist for jacket: A. J. Battifarano. Photographer's assistant: Salvatore Maiuro.